John Paul Jackson

Inheriting the Fullness
of God's Names

John Paul Jackson
I AM: Inheriting the Fullness of God's Names
Copyright © 2003 by John Paul Jackson

Requests for information should be addressed to:
Streams Publications
P.O. Box 550
North Sutton, NH 03260
Tel: (603) 927-4224
Web site: www.streamsministries.com

Scripture references marked NASB are from the New American Standard Bible, copyrighted by the Lockman Foundation, 1960, 1962, 1963, 1971, 1972, 1975, 1977, and are used with permission.

Unless otherwise indicated, all Scripture quotations are taken from The Holy Bible, New King James Version. Copyright © 1979, 1980, 1982 by Thomas Nelson, Inc.

ISBN: 1-58483-037-9

Printed in the United States of America.

To God,
who never changes.

Contents

✦

Acknowledgments

✦

Although my name appears on the cover of this book, I have a large and gifted team that has contributed significantly to its development. The presence of my wife, Diane, can be seen and felt throughout this book and in all that I do.

Carolyn Blunk served as creative director and managing editor, helping to shape this book for maximum impact. Associate editor, Jordan Bateman, helped significantly with the writing of this book. David Trementozzi offered assistance in the early stages of this book. A special thanks goes to Dorian Kreindler and Roxanne Stewart for meticulously copyediting the manuscript. Zach Mapes assisted with the production of this book. Also working inconspicuously behind the scenes were friends who took time out from their schedules to proofread the manuscript: Don Archibald, Paul and Pat Leary, Diana Woods, and D. J. Van Iwaarden. The rest of my staff did everything in their power to streamline my duties so that I would have time to write.

Preface

To guide you in your study of inheriting the fullness of God's names, I have included this list of 365 names and attributes of God, each recorded in Scripture, and compiled in *I AM: 365 Names of God*. This book, available from Streams Ministries, divides the names into twelve categories, and is a wonderful devotional tool. Each I AM comes with a Bible verse where the name or attribute can be found.

God of Wonders

I AM the God who shows wonders.
I AM the Lord, and My voice is powerful and full of majesty.
I AM God; nothing is too hard for Me.
I AM God, who made all My wonderful works to be remembered.
I AM God, and My glory thunders.
I AM the Spirit of knowledge and understanding.
I AM the Holy Spirit who moved upon the deep.
I AM worthy of worship, glorious and incomparable.
I AM God, who makes Himself known through visions.
I AM dunamis power.
I AM the giver of all revelation.
I AM glorious and full of weighty splendor.
I AM He who ascended to the Father.
I AM the Triune God of Israel.
I AM God, who performs signs.
I AM God, who speaks in night seasons.
I AM the King of glory.
I AM He who searches the mind and heart.
I AM great and greatly to be praised.
I AM Yah and Yahweh.
I AM the Creator of all true worship.
I AM wisdom.
I AM omniscient.
I AM the Lord, who stretches out the Heavens.
I AM God, who speaks.
I AM Jehovah-Rapha, your healer.
I AM God, who declares new things before they spring forth.
I AM the answer of your tongue.
I AM prophecy fulfilled, never early, never late.
I AM God, who gives you dreams.
I AM above all who are thought to be gods.

God of Symbols

I AM found in My appointed feasts.
I AM the anointing oil.
I AM the bright cloud that comes to you.
I AM the synagogue, church, tabernacle, and temple.
I AM the living water of life.
I AM the shofar trumpet.
I AM the fountain of Israel.
I AM Israel's living star.
I AM the Passover.
I AM the Ark of the Covenant.
I AM the door.
I AM the altar of the tabernacle.
I AM the balm of Gilead.
I AM the rose of Sharon.
I AM the tree of life.
I AM the God of Bethel.
I AM the lily of the valley.
I AM God, whose Sabbaths are a sign between you and Me.
I AM the rainbow's color.
I AM the Rock; there is no other.
I AM the glory in the cloud of the temple.
I AM the bread of life.
I AM your Rock, full of living water.
I AM the light of the world.
I AM a consuming fire.
I AM the north, your promoter.
I AM the bright and Morning Star.
I AM the light — luminous, glowing, and radiant One.

God of Mercy

I AM God, who is merciful.
I AM favor, and I grant favor to whom I choose.
I AM God of the spotted and speckled.
I AM the Prince of Peace, prophesied by the prophet Isaiah.
I AM God, who restores your soul.
I AM the friend of sinners.
I AM God, I tempt no one.
I AM the God of peace.
I AM He who weeps with those who weep.
I AM He who speaks from a position of mercy.
I AM long suffering.
I AM My Spirit.
I AM gracious.
I AM the forgiver of all transgressions.
I AM the manna that came down from Heaven.
I AM the breath that gives you life.
I AM He who will not remember your sins.
I AM the beloved in the Song of Songs.
I AM God, who stretches out His hand.
I AM the liberty you seek through My Spirit.
I AM ever faithful.
I AM God in the midst of your land.
I AM the forgiver of iniquity.
I AM abundant in mercy.
I AM the altar of peace for your fear.
I AM the Lord, who makes wise the simple.
I AM God, who is daily full of new mercy.
I AM God, who comforts you.
I AM God of the poor and the stranger.
I AM gentle and lowly in heart.
I AM the Lord, who exercises loving kindness.

God of Sacrifice

I AM the Christ.
I AM the cup of the blood.
I AM the eternal sacrifice.
I AM the blood that cleanses you from sin.
I AM the crucified Messiah of Calvary.
I AM your righteousness.
I AM the Yom Kippur offering to expiate all sins.
I AM worthy to open and read the scroll.
I AM Noah's Ark in a world still filled with sin.
I AM the wine and the bread.
I AM alive forevermore.
I AM the sprinkled blood of the Lamb on the doorposts of Israel.
I AM the door to the Father.
I AM the Lord, who rescues those with a contrite spirit.
I AM God's Son, sent to be seen face-to-face.
I AM He who left Heaven for you.
I AM your sanctification.
I AM the blood atonement.
I AM God's only Son.
I AM eternally blind to what I've forgiven.
I AM the bread of life, broken for you.
I AM He who blots out your transgressions.
I AM supplication.
I AM the pierced Messiah.
I AM the Keeper of the keys to hades and death.
I AM the God of your salvation.
I AM the Lamb that was slain.
I AM Father, Son, and Holy Spirit.
I AM outside the camp; come to Me.
I AM the way, the truth, and the life.

God of Justice

I AM the righteous judge of all creation.

I AM the King of Kings.

I AM with the generation of the righteous.

I AM God; My statutes rejoice the heart.

I AM the One who makes unbreakable covenants with mankind.

I AM holy, pure, and undefiled.

I AM God: besides Me there is no god.

I AM God by whom all actions are weighed.

I AM God: My testimony is sure.

I AM God: My commandments enlighten the eyes.

I AM the witness on your behalf.

I AM righteous; kings humble themselves before Me.

I AM God, whose eyelids test the sons of men.

I AM the Spirit of wisdom.

I AM My ordinances.

I AM the divine Judge of all things.

I AM the law.

I AM My statutes: walk in them.

I AM Judge of the living and the dead.

I AM the Spirit of the fear of the Lord.

I AM righteous.

I AM perfect knowledge.

I AM before whom every tongue will confess.

I AM the Lord, who loves righteousness.

I AM the unbiased, impartial Judge.

I AM the Lord and My judgments are righteous altogether.

I AM He who sent Moses to deliver Israel.

I AM God, and no one can reverse My acts.

I AM to be feared above all gods.

I AM God, who refines you.

I AM My judgments.

I AM the Lord who heals you.

God of Promise

I AM returning.

I AM God, and I want you to believe in Me.

I AM He who places your tears in My bottle, in My book.

I AM God, who shows you things to come.

I AM the seven Spirits, and they are Me.

I AM the Lord; the fear of Me is a fountain of life.

I AM God; My secrets are with those who fear Me.

I AM life's guarantor of joy and health.

I AM God, who will be found by those who seek Me with all their heart and soul.

I AM, and you shall know My names.

I AM He who leads you in the paths of righteousness.

I AM the architect of the last days.

I AM the sole key-giver of Heaven.

I AM the God who hears.

I AM the Lord, who hears those who speak about My name.

I AM God, who leads you to prophesy.

I AM the soon-coming King.

I AM the Lord; I do not change.

I AM always with you, wherever you are.

I AM God, who speaks through dreams.

I AM God, who reveals His form.

I AM the healing you seek.

I AM the Savior who will descend on the Mount of Olives.

I AM God, who gives you visions.

I AM God of those who are growing old.

I AM coming quickly.

I AM the One coming on the white horse.

I AM the soon-rending of the Heavens.

I AM the precision of My Scripture.

I AM waiting for you.

God the Shepherd

I AM your shepherd; you shall not want.

I AM the rod that chastises and brings you comfort.

I AM in the desert wilderness to be tender with you.

I AM near to those who have a broken heart.

I AM your confidence.

I AM compassion.

I AM in the Father.

I AM with you and will keep you wherever you go.

I AM the refuge of the poor.

I AM your Father.

I AM God in the stillness.

I AM the Lord; he who is joined with Me is one spirit with Me.

I AM the Spirit of counsel.

I AM your provider.

I AM tenderness.

I AM the true Shepherd.

I AM the dispeller of all fear and doubt.

I AM interceding for you right now.

I AM love.

I AM the staff that retrieves you.

I AM humanity's friend who sticks closer than a brother.

I AM the shepherd's rod.

I AM God, who is with you in the valley of the shadow of death.

I AM there with you.

I AM God, who strengthens you.

I AM the candle lighting your path.

I AM the Lord; precious in My sight is the death of all My saints.

I AM the Counselor, Mighty God, Everlasting Father.

I AM your peace and calm.

I AM He who wipes away your tears.

I AM the saving refuge of My anointed.

God the Ancient One

I AM the Lord God of Abraham, Isaac, and Jacob.

I AM the Holy Spirit, who hovered over the chaos of this earth.

I AM the light of Genesis that was before light was.

I AM the sacred Shema of the ancients.

I AM the Holy One of Israel.

I AM the One whose ways are perfect.

I AM God; the fear of Me is clean, enduring forever.

I AM the Holy of Holies.

I AM the God of knowledge.

I AM the Lord, sitting on His throne.

I AM God, who formed the earth to be inhabited.

I AM understanding.

I AM God, who is joined to the eunuch.

I AM the God of all the holy prophets in Scripture.

I AM God, who divided the sea.

I AM the Lord of the dance.

I AM the Lord.

I AM the guiding star at Jesus' birth.

I AM God, who turns water into wine.

I AM He of whom all the prophets foretold.

I AM the Root of the Offspring of David.

I AM God, who leads you into all truth.

I AM God, whose rainbow is My everlasting covenant with you.

I AM the Root of Jesse.

I AM the God of Jerusalem, wherein is My name.

I AM the Creator of Israel.

I AM the God, who divided the waters.

I AM the fountain of the house of David.

I AM God, who shuts up the Heavens.

I AM God, who turns water into blood.

I AM married to Israel.

God the Reward

I AM your exceedingly great reward.

I AM the Lord; taste and see that I am good.

I AM both the giver and the gifts.

I AM the preparer of your place in Heaven.

I AM able to give you much more than this.

I AM the one source of all true wealth.

I AM the Spirit of liberty.

I AM He who anoints your head with oil.

I AM the Bridegroom returning for My bride.

I AM the Lord who looks on those who tremble at My Word.

I AM God, who prepares a table for you in the presence of your enemies.

I AM in the midst of two or three gathered in My name.

I AM God, who will answer you.

I AM the glory who conceals a matter for a king to search out.

I AM the fountain of gardens.

I AM the resurrection of My beloved.

I AM God, whose throne is in Heaven.

I AM from above.

I AM the Lord, whose countenance beholds the upright.

I AM the just rewarder of all who seek Me.

I AM God, who teaches you to profit.

I AM the giver of abundant life.

I AM more than you can ask or think.

I AM sitting at the right hand of the Father.

I AM the Maker of many mansions therein.

I AM the Sabbath rest.

I AM the inheritance of the Levite.

I AM the fountain of life.

I AM the giver of great wisdom.

I AM the Holy Spirit who hovers over your life to bring higher order.

God the Warrior

I AM the battle standard.
I AM your sharp two-edged sword.
I AM your battle cry.
I AM a warrior, and My Kingdom is spread by force.
I AM the Lord, mighty in battle.
I AM the One who annihilated Satan's plans.
I AM the Spirit of might.
I AM the master planner of all nations and kingdoms.
I AM He who leads you for My great name's sake.
I AM the conqueror of death, hell, and the grave.
I AM both warrior and poet.
I AM the Supreme God, deliverer, and possessor.
I AM the Lord of Hosts.
I AM the Kingdom, the power, and the glory.
I AM God, who cast out nations before you.
I AM commander-in-chief of all Heaven's armies.
I AM He who drives out the wicked before you.
I AM the defender of those who believe in Me.
I AM your strength.
I AM the Lamb sitting on the throne.
I AM your victorious banner.
I AM the fullness of greatness, power, glory, victory, and majesty.
I AM God Almighty and infinite in strength.
I AM your mighty shield.
I AM the Lion of the tribe of Judah.
I AM the sword of the Spirit.
I AM your high tower.
I AM the defender of Israel.
I AM your fortress.
I AM omnipotent.
I AM the enemy of the enemies of Israel.

God of Eternity

I AM: I never change.

I AM the first and the last.

I AM one.

I AM humanity's builder of faith through the ages.

I AM ruler of both the night and the day.

I AM the uncaused, eternal, self-existent One.

I AM King forever and ever.

I AM Spirit.

I AM the Alpha and the Omega.

I AM God, whose eyes behold.

I AM the same every day.

I AM the Word of Life, called the Bible.

I AM the cornerstone.

I AM the resurrection and the life.

I AM not of this world.

I AM God, who knows all My works through eternity.

I AM omnipresent.

I AM the One who simultaneously sees beginning and end.

I AM God, ready to perform My word.

I AM three-in-one, equal and eternal.

I AM before the day was.

I AM all My names.

I AM the self-sufficient, self-sustaining, self-creating One.

I AM God; there is no other.

I AM the Word, which was in the beginning.

I AM the Rock of Ages on which you stand.

I AM He who was, and is, and is to come.

I AM Who I Am.

I AM the everlasting God.

I AM He who inhabits eternity.

God of Every Creature

I AM the Lord; the fear of Me is the beginning of wisdom.

I AM the God of multiplication and reproduction.

I AM Jehovah, that is My name.

I AM the God of the seraphim.

I AM the God of the cherubim.

I AM the God of all flesh.

I AM the vine.

I AM the artist from whom all artisans draw.

I AM Adonai Eloheynu; there is none other.

I AM the foundation of the world.

I AM invisible, yet all creation speaks of Me.

I AM God; I want you to understand and know Me.

I AM, and you are My witnesses.

I AM glorified in you.

I AM God, who made you a sign to the unbeliever.

I AM more than all structures of steel, mortar, and clay.

I AM jealous for you.

I AM the exalted head over all.

I AM God, who is joined to the foreigner.

I AM God, who speaks face-to-face.

I AM the sovereign ruler of all creation.

I AM your next breath.

I AM the light of the world.

I AM God, and all that is in Heaven and in earth is Mine.

I AM Immanuel, God dwelling among us.

I AM high and lifted up by all creation.

I AM the outpoured Spirit on all flesh.

I AM He who rejoices with those who rejoice.

I AM the only creator of all that exists.

I AM Savior of both the Gentiles and the Jews.

I AM He before whom every knee will bow.

Introduction

✛

Now the Lord descended in the cloud and stood with him there, and proclaimed the name of the Lord. And the Lord passed before him and proclaimed, "The Lord, the Lord God, merciful and gracious, longsuffering, and abounding in goodness and truth, keeping mercy for thousands, forgiving iniquity and transgression and sin, by no means clearing the guilty, visiting the iniquity of the fathers upon the children and the children's children to the third and the fourth generation." So Moses made haste and bowed his head toward the earth, and worshipped. —Exodus 34:5-8

God's name is our heritage, our authority, our hope. It is our very life essence — a part of God's glory we need desperately. His name, and the fullness that comes with it, must be seared into our very being. To carry it properly, we must have character above reproach, standing pure and holy before Him. It's a huge task, but one with a glorious reward. My prayer is that this book, *I AM: Inheriting the Fullness of God's Names*, will help you in that journey.

To get the most out of this book, you need the first book in this series, *I AM: 365 Names of God*. That work collects 365 names and characteristics of God, putting them into 12 categories for easy study. Each page includes a name and the Scripture in which that name is found. It has been a powerful devotional tool for thousands of people, giving them a broad understanding of the name, acts, and glory of the Lord. I suggest that while reading this book, *I AM: Inheriting the Fullness of God's Names*, you meditate on one of the names found in *I AM: 365 Names of God* every day. Record your thoughts and prayers in a journal. God wants to unveil your eyes and show you the mystery and majesty of His name.

I AM: 365 Names of God was a labor of love for me. It's a book I have always wanted to write and publish. It was written for an audience of One. As my staff and I put it together, I told the Lord that I was doing it only for Him. Even if every copy I printed was left untouched in my warehouse forever, I knew it was important to write the book. It was an act of worship — a gesture of love for a God who saved me from death. I wanted to honor and glorify His name.

That audience of One, in His graciousness, has released the first I AM to thousands of people around the world. Because of that, I felt compelled to add a second volume to the series. The book you now hold in your hands will teach you how to fully embrace the names of God and inherit the blessings that come with them.

This book includes an interactive feature called Reflection Questions. At the end of each chapter, I have added questions meant to spark meditation, thought, and prayer by the reader. I encourage you to pause when these questions are asked, pray about them, and answer honestly. In fact, I suggest you start a journal and write down your answers and thoughts to these questions. When you have finished answering one, quiet yourself once again. Ask the Lord to give you His answer to the same question — you might be surprised by what you hear. If the answers about your life and relationship with Him differ, ask Him to heal your perspective and give you fresh eyes to see things as He does.

Each chapter concludes with a suggested Scripture reading. Reading your Bible is the best way to learn God's names and have His character poured into you. He reveals Himself through His Scripture, especially through His names. We, as Christians, must read it diligently and carefully. It truly is our daily bread. Without it, the gifts, even the deepest revelatory gifts, starve and wither away. Each Bible study includes thought-provoking questions. Again, I suggest you study the passages with a journal handy. Write down the revelation God gives you through His Word. What lessons is He teaching you? What can you learn about God's nature and names through the passage? The greatest lessons I have learned about the Lord and His glory have come through an intimate study of His Bible.

It is my dream that this book will teach you how to make decisions and live a lifestyle that justifies God acting on your behalf. When you make a decision, make it the one that creates the conditions which allow God to act on your behalf. His names guarantee the provision for our justification. Learning His names changes our thought life, which in turn will change our actions. Our actions become our habits, and our habits become our destiny. Thus, our very destiny is changed by learning His names. By leaning on His wisdom, His power, and His names' authority, we live in a way that other people will want to emulate.

Our anointing becomes greater, because God's names become greater in our lives. Soon you will find yourself growing to expect God to be true to Himself, to bear witness, as the Bible says, to His name. You will pray with faith and favor, believing that God is still truly God, and that He will answer your prayer. Your love for Him will be vindicated again and again, and His name will shine brightly over your life and circumstances. Where hope and expectancy collide, faith is the spiritual product. Hope in His name, expect Him to act according to His ways, and faith will be birthed in your life. Faith that God will be true to His name is the key to unlocking the whole realm of the miraculous.

That's why I'm so excited about this book. If Christians began to truly believe in God's names and the acts and glory that come with them, the Church would be quickly revitalized. Healings would occur in massive numbers. Prophetic voices would spring up loudly and boldly. The lost would be saved like snow falling in winter. God's names are *that* powerful.

Our hope and our expectancy have to touch at such a level that faith can be generated. That's when miracles happen, because it creates a mixture irresistible to God and the glory of His name. Meditate on His names. Ponder them. Love them. Absorb them. Incorporate them into your life. Worship God for them. The more you do this, the more momentum you will gain spiritually. God wants to give you the power of His names — as long as your character proves you will reciprocate by giving Him all the glory for it.

We are all partakers of the divine nature. Let us bear God's names boldly and purely, for the sake of His Kingdom, and the lost He dreams of saving.

John Paul Jackson

❖

chapter One

Hallowed Be Your Name

Simon Peter, James and John the sons of Zebedee, Andrew, Philip, Bartholomew, Thomas, Matthew, James the son of Alphaeus, Thaddaeus, Simon the Canaanite, and Judas Iscariot are among the most influential men ever to walk this planet. Jesus had given everything to them — His life, His authority, and His vision. More than that, He had given them His friendship, His companionship, and His care.

Jesus loved these twelve roughneck, oft-stubborn men, and held nothing back from them. In their presence, He had healed the sick, fed thousands, raised the dead, prophesied the future, and done countless other miracles. He had answered their questions and shared the secrets of the universe. They were more than His friends; they were His brothers. Still, there was one habit of Jesus' these twelve disciples wanted to emulate more than any other; one secret they wanted to learn from Him was how to pray.

One day, one of the disciples asked, "Lord, teach us to pray" (Luke 11:1). Jesus did, in a passage that has become one of the most recited in Scripture, the Lord's Prayer (Matthew 6:9-13):

> Our Father in heaven, hallowed be Your name. Your kingdom come. Your will be done on earth as it is in heaven. Give us this day our daily bread. And forgive us our debts, as we forgive our debtors. And do not lead us into temptation, but deliver us from the evil one. For Yours is the kingdom and the power and the glory forever. Amen.

The first sentence of the Lord's Prayer serves not only as the foundation for the entire passage, but as the very foundation of His blessing in our lives. Jesus began by saying, "Our Father in heaven, hallowed be Your name."

Essentially, Jesus was teaching us that we need to pause and revere God's name in our hearts. We need to meditate on how holy and pure His name is. We need to treat His name with such honor that it becomes branded in our minds and embedded in our lifestyles. Jesus knew that if we hallowed God's name in this way, people would see the Spirit of the Living God resting upon our lives.

As Christians, we have recited the Lord's Prayer hundreds of times, but have we stopped to consider the words Jesus used? Have we hallowed every aspect, attribute, or facet of the name of God?

To completely embrace the Lord's name, we must come to a

fundamental understanding of the biblical context surrounding the phrase "hallowed be Your name." To do that, we must understand the Hebrew mind-set surrounding the mystique of a given name.

Hebrew Understanding

Many of us today do not place much significance in a name. Millions of children are named every year, with little thought given to the historic and spiritual meaning of their names. For many Christians, the only time they are confronted by the meaning of their name is when they see their name on little parchment scrolls along with a two-word explanation and a Bible verse sitting on a Christian bookstore rack. They read Proverbs all their life, but don't give a second thought to pieces of wisdom like "A good name is to be chosen rather than great riches," (Proverbs 22:1).

Yet that simple proverb gives us a valuable glimpse into what Solomon and the ancient Israelites thought about the value of a name. In Hebrew culture, as recorded in the Old Testament, the word *name (shem)* meant "a mark of individuality; [with] implications of honor, authority, and character" (*Strong's,* Hebrew section, p. 117). In the Bible, a name often provided an important clue to the nature of a person or place.

The ancient Hebrew understanding of a person's name was inseparably linked to the concept of character. Quite simply, one's name was reputation. During Old Testament times, to honor and revere a name, to hallow it, was equivalent to showing honor and respect for the person and all that he or she represented.

Furthermore, the name of a child was often descriptive of the parents' dreams and expectations for the child. Children were named with the hope that they would aspire to the significance of what their name meant.

For example, if a boy's mother and father named him *David*, which means "beloved," they hoped the baby would grow to be a person who was loved by God and people. In naming a child, many Israelites believed that a name had the ability to influence the child's destiny.

Jesus carried on this tradition in the New Testament, when he renamed His friend Simon.

> Jesus answered and said to him, "Blessed are you, Simon Bar-Jonah, for flesh and blood has not revealed this to you, but My Father who is in heaven. And I also say to you that you are Peter, and on this rock I will build My Church, and the gates of Hades shall not prevail against it." —MATTHEW 16:17-18

Jesus took the name *Peter*, from *petros*, the Greek word for "rock," and gave it to His friend as a prophetic word of Simon's call and future in the Kingdom of God.

It wasn't the first time God had changed the name of one of His friends. God spoke to Abram:

> No longer shall your name be called Abram, but your name shall be Abraham; for I have made you a father of many nations. —GENESIS 17:5

Two generations later, God renamed Abraham's grandson Jacob:

> Your name shall no longer be called Jacob, but Israel; for you have struggled with God and with men, and have prevailed. —GENESIS 32:28

Name changes were made as a sign of the covenants God made with the patriarchs.

Throughout Scripture, God uses names as windows of revelation into the character of men and women. The Bible is littered with examples: Nabal the fool: "For as his name is, so is he: Nabal is his name, and folly is with him," (1 Samuel 25:25); Eve the mother of all: "And Adam called his wife's name Eve, because she was the mother of all living," (Genesis 3:20); Isaiah's children: Shear-Jashub, meaning "A remnant will return," (Isaiah 7:3); Maher-Shalal-Hash-Baz, meaning "Speed the spoil," (Isaiah 8:1-3); even the tower of Babel: "Therefore its name is called Babel, because there the Lord confused the language of all the earth; and from there the Lord scattered them abroad over the face of all the earth," (Genesis 11:9).

If human names were this important to God, the creator of all symbols and metaphors, how much more vital must be His own name? Just imagine the depth of character contained in the hundreds of names God has ordained for Himself. No wonder we are called to hallow His name!

Yahweh and YHWH

For millennia, Israelites fostered such a reverence for God's name that the practice developed of avoiding its use. In revealing Himself to Abraham, God had used the name *Yahweh*, but the name was thought too holy to pronounce, or to record. That's why most Bibles are littered with footnotes that say simply *"YHWH."* Ancient scribes were uncomfortable recording God's full name, so they left part of it out. Others began to use another name by which God had revealed Himself, Adonai, translated as "Lord."

Each of the names of God, which He has seeded into Scripture, reveal an aspect of God's character and His relationship with us. These names are to be hallowed for what they are: examples of God's glory and reputation. In sharing His name, God offers Himself as a Person in order to bring Himself into relationship with humankind. Not only is God revealing Himself in a personal way, but, according to the biblical concept of a name, He is also revealing His character and reputation to humankind.

In Exodus 3, we read how God, speaking through the burning bush, announced His name to Moses as "I AM WHO I AM" (Exodus 3:14). This is a declaration of God's self-existence. Later, God added to Moses' knowledge about Him by proclaiming His name and listing the various facets of His character:

> The Lord, the Lord God, merciful and gracious, longsuffering, and abounding in goodness and truth, keeping mercy for thousands, forgiving iniquity and transgression and sin, by no means clearing the guilty, visiting the iniquity of the fathers upon the children and the children's children to the third and the fourth generation. —Exodus 34:6-7

The same principle worked for Abram, who later became Abraham. When the Lord appeared to Abram in a vision, He promised His protection: "Do not be afraid, Abram. I am your shield, your exceedingly great reward" (Genesis 15:1). God later identified Himself further: "I am the Lord [Yahweh] who brought you out of Ur of the Chaldeans, to give you this land to inherit it" (Genesis 15:7). These names, these qualities, taught Abraham much about the nature of his greatest friend.

In the Israelite context, one could confer one's own name upon another person, place, or thing. When this was done, the latter came under the person's influence and protection. Consequently, in God making known His name, He was giving humankind the opportunity to receive the protection, blessing, and covering that His name provides. What is the significance of all this? Two things: it is an invitation for relationship and an invitation to ask for protection and blessing.

An Invitation for Relationship

First, God's desire to be known in a personal way reveals an important aspect of His character. He wants to enter into a relationship with His creation. Unlike the pagan deities of ancient history, whom myths portrayed as afraid to reveal their names lest humankind should exert power over them, God invites any and all to call out His name and experience the blessings it will bring.

It is truly remarkable that the eternally self-sustaining Creator would desire to become part of the very world He made. He took on a name so that He could be known and loved by His creation.

Nowhere is God's desire for relationship more evident than in His decision to send His Son, Jesus, to earth. Jesus told Nicodemus:

> For God so loved the world that He gave His only begotten Son, that whoever believes in Him should not perish but have everlasting life. —JOHN 3:16

God's name was carried boldly and completely by Jesus, as an example to us of how we can have relationship with the Father.

An Invitation for Protection and Blessing

Not only does God offer us the blessing of knowing Him personally, but He also offers us the blessing of reaping the benefits of influence, favor, and protection that His name brings. God is the

King of all the earth. As such, He offers us the eternal protection
and blessing of His name, both in this life and in the life to come.
All we need to do is simply believe in His name. In the New
Testament, we are told that if we call upon the name of the Lord,
we will experience the saving power of God, both physically and
spiritually (Acts 2:21).

God loves to draw close to His children and give them the
benefits of His name. God promised the Israelites:

> In every place where 1 record My name 1 will come to you,
> and 1 will bless you. —Exodus 20:24

Misusing God's Name

Only as we step outside of the modern-day understanding of names,
and the flippancy so commonly associated with them, can we
understand the importance of keeping the third commandment:

> You shall not take the name of the Lord your God in vain,
> for the Lord will not hold him guiltless who takes His
> name in vain. —Exodus 20:7

Grave consequences exist for those who misuse God's name. His
name has been used wrongly in false religions, magic, in profanity,
and in substantiating truth through the use of oaths.

By speaking God's name, the Israelites understood that awesome
and awful power would be released against God's enemies, that
miracles would occur, and that He would appear with His terrifying
glorious presence. God's name was like no other, a name deserving
the utmost honor, reverence, and respect. His name, above all others,
deserved to be hallowed.

God's intention of blessing His people by teaching them rightly to honor and revere His name brought a fear of misusing it. Consequently, God-fearing Jews took on the practice of never even uttering the name Yahweh.

Although He wants us to treat Him with a holy fear, God doesn't want us to be afraid of His name. In fact, He wants us desperately to call out His name so that it can become a shield of protection and an open storehouse of blessing for us. God wants to give us His name. He calls us His children, and all children bear the names of their parents. To be called His child is a sign of great endearment and love.

God yearns to put His name on us, but He will only do so with those who have learned rightly to hallow and revere it.

✤ Reflection Questions ✤

1. God's name is plural in nature. Why do you suppose Jesus said we need to hallow God's name?

2. What does this mean in modern language?

3. How can we hallow the name of God in our lives?

4. What does your name mean? (If you need help, check websites like www.behindthename.com or www.babynames.com, or try a baby name book.)

5. Where did your parents get your name? Were they going to name you something else?

6. How does the meaning of your name fit with your character and your life?

7. What does it mean to be a child of God?

8. How does His name affect your relationship with Him?

9. Have you ever desperately called on the name of God to save you? What happened?

✤ Recommended Scripture Reading ✤

Exodus 3 and 4: Moses and the Burning Bush

⌢ What does God reveal about Himself in this passage?

⌢ What does God think about Moses trying to wriggle his way out of God's plan?

⌢ How does Moses' family react to God's call on his life?

✦

chapter Two

People Who Know Their God

An important part of hallowing the name of God is learning how to bear His name in our lives. We must desire, more than anything else, to be marked by God's name. His name must replace every ounce of our selfish, soulish beings so that we might be conformed to His nature. Only then will the Holy Spirit hover in and through our lives, for He is only comfortable in places where He is welcomed — places that are branded by His name.

Horace, the Shoe Shiner

One day while sitting in an airport, I felt the Lord impressing me to wait in line for a young man named Horace who was shining shoes.

As I watched Horace humbly polish the shoes of different businessmen, God opened my spiritual eyes, and I saw the Spirit of the Lord resting upon him. In my spirit, I discerned that Horace loved Jesus Christ very, very much.

Then my turn arrived. As Horace began to polish my shoes, he gazed up at me and said, "You have the Spirit of God on you."

"Horace, I was just going to tell you the same thing!" I said with amazement. "You have the Spirit of God resting on you. Horace, you are going to be a great man of God one day. You may be shining shoes now, but the Lord has plans for your life. In fact, Horace, there is healing in your hands right now — these very hands that are shining my shoes."

As I prophesied about how God wanted to bless Horace, tears filled his eyes and streamed down his cheeks. God's Spirit was resting on this young man working in an airport. God's name of healing, Jehovah-Rapha, was powerfully written on his life.

The Name of God and the Anointing of God

Over the years, many books have been written about the anointing of God. It is an important part of a healthy Christian walk, as the anointing is the manifestation of God's names expressed in an individual. It comes as the result of a name of God being placed upon our lives.

God's names, His acts, and His glory are all inseparable. His names describe who He is throughout the ages, and they describe what He has done and will do. For example, God, who was once Jehovah-Rapha, is not now ex-Jehovah-Rapha. He is *still* Jehovah-Rapha, the God who heals. God didn't lose His power to heal when the last apostle died. He didn't lose His power to heal when the

Bible was canonized. He was, He is, and He will be continually Jehovah-Rapha.

Pillar of Fire or Wisp of Smoke?

Once, God illustrated this point to me in a vision where I saw people marching through a valley surrounded by mountains. As the people came closer into view, I noticed their formation was very dense. In incredible unity, they seemed like a penetrating, concise laser beam as they marched down the valley floor. A huge flame, so large it looked like a cloud, advanced before them as they walked with purpose and focus. They were a formidable army, led by a powerful manifestation of God's presence.

Enemy kings, who were standing along the mountainsides, looked down into the valley. Their knees trembled as they saw the supernatural, cloudlike flame rising into the Heavens. Knowing they faced an incredibly potent army, the enemy kings tried to hide their fear as they issued commands to their troops. In their heart, they knew this battle was a lost cause, for they were about to wage war against God Himself.

God's glory was marching before the approaching army. From the biblical record of the Israelites' journey through the Sinai Desert, we are told this pillar was a cloud by day and a fire by night. We are told this was the glory of God made manifest to, and leading, the children of Israel. With God before them, who could be against them?

Suddenly that vision passed, and another vision appeared. Once again, a group of people were coming down the valley floor, but they were scattered like pepper on the floor. Some walked up into the mountainsides. Some walked up ahead. Some walked to the side. And some lingered behind. This group was not walking in unison.

I scanned the valley desperately for the cloud and the pillar of fire that was supposed to lead them. As they came closer into view, I realized that the pillar was indeed there, but it appeared as a thin, threadlike wisp that was barely recognizable. The people's disbelief, dysfunction and disunity had allowed God's leadership in their lives to wither away.

As I looked along the mountainsides, I noticed the enemy looking down over the group of people. The enemy wasn't afraid. In fact, they seemed like vultures that had just spied an easy prey. They were licking their chops with excitement over their impending victory.

Then the Lord spoke to me. "Son, do you know what this is?"

"No," I replied.

"The first group was My people Israel when they came out of Egypt," the Lord explained. "The kings of the land saw them, and great fear fell upon them. My glory was with them. This second group of people is the Church today. They have reduced My glory to a thin wisp of smoke, and they wonder why the kings of the earth don't tremble when they come near."

Puzzled, I asked, "How have we reduced Your name to a thinlike wisp of smoke?"

The Lord then began to speak to me about His name. He said, "You have reduced the manifested measure of My glory, because you have caused My name, My acts, and My glory to be separated."

"My name is Jehovah-Rapha," the Lord continued. "I am the God Who Heals. I didn't used to heal. I still heal. Many of My people say 'God no longer heals.' As a result, they have removed a means by which I receive glory. An aspect of My glory is gone from them."

The Lord continued to explain how we have removed various other means by which He receives glory. We strip Him of His glory by saying that His attributes no longer exist today. For example, some say that God no longer predicts the future. So they take this aspect of His name and place it to the side. Others say that God no longer delivers. Or that God no longer sanctifies, because they believe there is no longer a need for a sanctified life. Every Christian, at some point in his or her life, has deleted or distorted pieces of God's incredible glory, casting it aside like an old, worn-out cloak. And the Church is weaker for it.

Finally, the Lord said, "When these different aspects of My name are rejected, and the people say that I no longer do those things My name says, then what is left is a threadlike wisp of smoke. My acts, My name, and My glory are inseparable."

In his beloved classic, *Knowing God*, J. I. Packer wrote that "Ignorance of God, ignorance of both His ways and of the practice of communion with Him, lies at the root of much of the Church's weakness today." Such ignorance "spawns great thoughts of man and leaves room for only small thoughts of God."

What are the effects of knowing and honoring God's names? In the book of Daniel we read, "the people who know their God will display strength and take action" (Daniel 11:32, NASB). Knowing God's names, character, and attributes are aspects of knowing Him.

The Indivisibility of God's Name, Acts, and Glory

We need to understand that God is glorious because He does what no one else, in Heaven or on earth, can do. When we reject or fail to recognize what He does, we have thrown away His glory because God's glory is linked to His activity. God's glory is not separate from the acts that His names reveal. His glory is His acts, and His acts are His name.

Therefore, Jehovah-Rapha is not only "the God Who Heals" but rather "God Is Healing" or "the God of Healing." Every fiber of His being is healing.

Likewise, every fiber of God's being is prophecy. Every fiber of His being is peace. Every fiber of His being is love. Every fiber of His being is light. Every fiber of His being is justice. Every fiber of His being is gracious. Every fiber of His being is contained in the fullest expression of every aspect of His name. Thus, God's acts and His names are inseparable.

God's acts do not just demonstrate His glory; they are His glory. Within the acts of God is found the glory of God. The acts of God — healing, deliverance, peace, provision, love — are manifestations of His glory. But in a literal sense, they are also His glory. His name, His acts, and His glory are inseparable.

Why is this important? When we pray "Our Father in heaven, hallowed be Your name," we are not simply hallowing a singular name for God. In this passage, the Greek word for *name* is plural. It means the composite combination of every possible name of God. Therefore, to hallow God's name means that we don't separate His name from His acts or His glory. We honor, revere, believe, and *amen* receive every aspect that His names express. We embrace the relevance, the nearness, and the accessibility of His names. We do not relegate them as names for different eras of time, such as a name for yesterday or a name for tomorrow. Instead, we inherit the fullness of His names on our behalf today. *amen*

God is not the God who used to do what His names depict. No! He is the God who still does all that His names encompass. *amen*

When we have difficulty embracing God's names, we have truly failed to believe and respond to all God says He is and does. We fail to experience the fullness of who He really is, and the miraculous, life-changing power of His glory.

Moreover, how can we hallow or revere a particular name of God if we no longer believe it expresses a present attribute of God? The definition of *hallow* is "to revere, respect, value, cherish, and honor." When Jesus taught us to pray by saying "hallowed be Your name," He was implying that we need to recognize the full attributes of God. If we call Him the God of healing but don't believe He actually heals today, we devalue God — the complete opposite of hallowing His name.

Furthermore, God's name represents something humankind can never be. We can only taste the essence of God's name. We do not have within ourselves the divine qualities that His name represents. For example, unless the God of peace dwells within us, we cannot know true peace. Unless the God of love dwells within us, we cannot truly love. We need His names, His acts, and His glory to reside within us. amen & amen

Did you ever wonder what Jesus meant when He prayed "I have manifested *Your name* to the men whom You have given Me..." (John 17:6)? Jesus manifested the God of Peace, Jehovah-Shalom, to His disciples. He manifested healing, Jehovah-Rapha, to them. He manifested sanctification, Jehovah-M'Kaddesh, to them. Jesus manifested all of the attributes of God to the world — His names.

In the Great Commission, Jesus released us to do all that He did (Matthew 28:16-20). As His followers, we are commanded to manifest the names of God: amen

Go into all the world and preach the gospel to every creature. He who believes and is baptized will be saved; but he who does not believe will be condemned. And

these signs will follow those who believe: In My name
they will cast out demons; they will speak with new
tongues; they will take up serpents; and if they drink
anything deadly, it will by no means hurt them; they
will lay hands on the sick, and they will recover.
—MARK 16:15-18

Jesus said, emphasizing that it was in His name that we would
receive power.

When we enter a meeting, we should expect the manifold
wisdom and presence of God to be there. Healing, deliverance,
salvation, peace, love, joy, wisdom, and all those things that make up
the names of God should be evidenced among believers, because they
should be bearing God's name, and by extension, His glory and acts.

If we desire to walk in the fullness of all God has for our lives,
then we must be convinced of the necessity of being marked by His
name. Only then will we be moved to take the necessary steps to
allow the Lord to place His name upon us.

God's name is precious. By the mere power of this name, all
healing springs forth. By the power of His name, all resources flow. By
the power of His name, all authority is conferred. Nothing on earth is
more important than bearing the name of our heavenly Father.

Since His name is so precious, God will not carelessly give it
away. Yet He offers it freely to any and all who so desire, to those who
have come to recognize its value and worth.

The prophet Malachi told of the joy God receives from those
who rightly honor His name.

Then those who feared the Lord spoke to one another, and
the Lord listened and heard them; So a book of

remembrance was written before Him for those who fear
the Lord and who meditate on His name. —MALACHI 3:16

You can almost picture the enjoyment God received from
listening to the conversations of those who feared and meditated on
His name. He loved it so much, He commanded a book of
remembrance be written in Heaven, honoring those who so rightly
honored Him. Like a favorite CD or movie, God can look back at any
instant to that book of remembrance and recall the pleasure of those
men and women worshipping His name. "Read that to me again,"
He can say to His angels and heavenly hosts. "I love that. One more
time, please," we can almost hear Him say. As Christians, we should
long to have our names and our worship recorded by God Himself.
We should hallow His name above all others. amen

That is the requirement: to cherish and desire His name more
than anything or anyone else. Once we are convinced of the power
and anointing contained in His names, we then must begin to act
upon it. The first step is simple — we must begin to learn and
meditate on His names.

✢ Reflection Questions ✢

1. Why should we bear the names of God in our lives?

2. What part of your life or nature would you like to exchange for God's purity?

3. How are you currently carrying God's name in your life, relationships, work, and ministry?

4. Have you ever had an experience with someone like Horace, who obviously bore the name of God in his or her life?

5. How did you feel when you were around this person?

6. How have you reduced God's glory through a lack of faith?

7. What have you forgotten to ask God for forgiveness? Ask Him to restore that quality in your life.

8. What is your favorite attribute of God? Take a moment to worship Him for it.

9. How will God remember your life?

10. What dreams does He have for you?

11. How many times has God written your name in His book of remembrance?

12. How can you get it entered more often?

✤ Recommended Scripture Reading ✤

Psalm 145: David Sings Praise to God.

‾ Make a list of the characteristics of God found in this passage.

‾ How are you "praising" God's works to the next generation, as verse 4 suggests we should do?

‾ Which verse especially resonates with your spirit? Why?

✛

chapter Three

The Name of the Lord Is a Strong Tower

As we understand the names of God, our eyes are opened to see His nature. Nowhere is God revealed as powerfully or as succinctly as in His names. When we know God, as He is, we are empowered to carry His name into every aspect of our lives.

Solomon wrote, "The name of the Lord is a strong tower; the righteous run to it and are safe" (Proverbs 18:10). Do you know the One who can protect you, who is your security from attack? Do you know what that name is?

Human language is incapable of expressing the fullness of God in a single name. Each year, the Hebrew high priest would pass God's name on to the next high priest — that name was only spoken once a year, and was about seventy-two Hebrew characters long. God is so powerful, so wise, and so amazing, that no single name could ever come close to capturing the magnificent greatness of who He is and what He does. Consequently, throughout the Bible, God made known to the children of Israel many names used to describe Himself. It is by these very names that He is known today.

Unfortunately, too many in the Church have become so familiar with God that they have ceased to remain awed by the wonder and glory of His majesty. Many have grown up knowing that God is awesome and mighty, but they have not been able to conceptualize how carrying God's name looks in the mundane realities of everyday life. Our familiarity with His name has bred contempt, an affront to God of terrible magnitude. We must repent of that sin, ask Him to forgive us, and again fear and love the name of God.

In the companion devotional to this book, *I AM: 365 Names of God*, I compiled a list of many of the names of God found in Scripture. I encourage you to get that book and begin meditating on those powerful names, asking God to brand you with them. The English word, *Lord*, is one word, but there are several words in the original languages of Scripture that we have simply translated to that one word. Here are a few I would like to highlight:

Jehovah-Tzidkenu

Jehovah-Tzidkenu: "The Lord Our Righteousness." God revealed this name to the prophet Jeremiah:

In His days Judah will be saved, and Israel will dwell

safely; Now this is His name by which He will be called: The Lord Our Righteousness. —JEREMIAH 23:6

Centuries later, the apostle Paul declared the astounding truth that God is the One who makes us free from guilt or sin.

For He made Him who knew no sin to be sin for us, that we might become the righteousness of God in Him. —2 CORINTHIANS 5:21

Jehovah-M'Kaddishchem

Jehovah-M'Kaddishchem: "The Lord Who Sanctifies You." Although God commands us to consecrate ourselves and to be holy, He makes us holy for His purposes. The Lord revealed this divine attribute to Moses:

You shall keep My statutes, and perform them: I am the Lord who sanctifies you. —LEVITICUS 20:8

Jehovah-Shalom

Jehovah-Shalom: "The Lord Is Peace." The book of Judges speaks of this name and attribute of God:

So Gideon built an altar there to the Lord, and called it The-Lord-Is-Peace. To this day it is still in Ophrah of the Abiezrites. —JUDGES 6:24

It was a theme the apostle Paul built upon:

For He Himself is our peace, who has made both one,
and has broken down the middle wall of separation..."
—EPHESIANS 2:14

Inner peace and freedom from anxiety comes by asking God, the
Lord Is Peace, to display this attribute in our lives.

Jehovah-Shammah

Jehovah-Shammah: "The Lord Is There." The prophet Ezekiel refers
to this name:

All the way around shall be eighteen thousand cubits;
and the name of the city from that day shall be: The Lord
Is There. —EZEKIEL 48:35

The great preacher Charles Spurgeon was also intrigued by this
name of God, and the importance of being where God is. "Even
Jerusalem, in its best estate, would have this for its crowning blessing:
nothing could exceed this," Spurgeon said. "Do we reckon the presence
of the Lord to be the greatest of blessings? Where we cannot enjoy God's
company we will not go. Our motto is: 'With God, anywhere. Without
God, nowhere.' In Him we live, and move, and have our being; and,
therefore, it would be death to us to be apart from God."

Jehovah-Rapha

Jehovah-Rapha: "The Lord Who Heals." The prophet Isaiah wrote
about the Lord:

But He was wounded for our transgressions, He was bruised

for our iniquities; the chastisement for our peace was upon Him, and by His stripes we are healed. —ISAIAH 53:5

Because Jesus was scourged unjustly, we can be healed. His blood was shed so The Lord Who Heals could minister to us.

Jehovah-Jireh

Jehovah-Jireh: "The Lord Will Provide." The book of Genesis says:

> Then Abraham lifted his eyes and looked, and there behind him was a ram caught in a thicket by its horns. So Abraham went and took the ram, and offered it up for a burnt offering instead of his son. And Abraham called the name of the place, "The-Lord-Will-Provide;" as it is said to this day, In the Mount of the Lord it shall be provided. —GENESIS 22:13-14

This is more than financial provision; it is a provision of everything we might need spiritually, physically, emotionally, and mentally. Jehovah-Jireh will provide all that we need.

Jehovah-Nissi

Jehovah-Nissi: "The Lord Is Our Victorious Banner." The apostle Paul described this attribute of God's name when he wrote:

> What then shall we say to these things? If God is for us, who can be against us? ...Yet in all these things we are more than conquerors through Him who loved us. —ROMANS 8:31, 37

The phrase "more than conquerors" is translated *hupernikao*, which means "over and above." It describes one who is made completely victorious.

Centuries earlier, Moses had seen God's power at work when the Israelites fought the Amalekites. When he lifted his arms, the Israelites advanced; when he let them down, the Amalekites recovered. Eventually, Aaron and Hur held Moses' arms up so the Israelites would be victorious. After the battle, Moses honored God. "And Moses built an altar and called its name, The-Lord-Is-My-Banner," Exodus 17:15 records.

Jehovah-Raah

Jehovah-Raah: "The Lord Is Our Shepherd." King David was one of the first to write on this attribute of God, in his beautiful Psalm 23: "The Lord is my shepherd; I shall not want." Jesus added to this when He said:

> My sheep hear My voice, and I know them, and they follow me: And I give them eternal life, and they shall never perish, neither shall anyone pluck them out of My hand. —JOHN 10:27-28

Jehovah-Nigad

Jehovah-Nigad: "The Lord Who Predicts the Future." In the book of Isaiah, God says:

> I am the Lord, that is My name. And My glory I will not

give to another, nor My praise to carved images. Behold, the former things have come to pass. New things I declare. Before they spring forth I tell you of them. —ISAIAH 42:8-9

Throughout Scripture, we read time and again that God reveals His future plans to His prophets and servants. He shares His plans with the ones He loves.

Jehovah-Ahavah

Jehovah-Ahavah: "God Is Love." It is God's nature to love (1 John 4:16). He keeps His covenant of love for a thousand generations with those who love Him and keep His commandments (Deuteronomy 7:9). In love, God reveals Himself to us and seeks fellowship with us. Love is a basic attribute of God's nature. He is the perfect expression of true love.

In all their affliction He was afflicted, and the Angel of His Presence saved them; in His love and in His pity He redeemed them; and He bore them and carried them all the days of old. —ISAIAH 63:9

Jehovah-Elohim

Jehovah-Elohim: "God Is Worthy of Worship." *Elohim* basically means something or someone that is worshipped. God told the Israelites that He was the true Elohim, the only One to be worshipped. The book of Genesis states:

This is the history of the heavens and the earth when they were created, in the day that the Lord God [Jehovah-Elohim] made the earth and the heavens. —Genesis 2:4

We see this characteristic of God's divine majesty and power in creation. Jehovah-Elohim sustains all that exists in the universe. God alone is the creator of all that exists and thus is worthy of our worship. There is nothing any man, woman, angel, demon, king, or queen can create apart from God. This creative God must then be worshipped, for He is truly unique.

Adonai

Adonai: "Lord." As our Maker, God holds rightful ownership of all humankind and therefore can rightly require our worship and obedience. He is Lord of all. When Abraham came to a point of surrender, He acknowledged that God was Lord of his life (Genesis 15:2, 8). Moses also yielded to God's lordship in Exodus 4:10-12 when he remembered that God was his Creator and could do all things. So must we each, individually, acknowledge God's ownership of our lives.

Jehovah-Qanna

Jehovah-Qanna: "The Lord Is Jealous." This aspect of God is repeatedly illustrated in the Old Testament as Israel continued to fall into cycles of forsaking God and worshipping idols. The Lord warned them:

You shall not make for yourself a carved image — any likeness of anything that is in heaven above, or that is in the earth beneath, or that is in the water under the earth; you shall not bow down to them nor serve them: for I, the Lord your God, am a jealous God, visiting the iniquity of the fathers upon the children to the third and fourth generation, of those who hate Me; but showing mercy to thousands, to those who love Me, and keep My commandments. —Exodus 20:4-6

Still, the Israelites were constantly tempted and succumbed to the worship of other gods. And the wrath of Jehovah-Qanna burned against them. What in our lives has become idols to us? What have we put before God in our own world? Are we fully submitted to His will? These are important questions to consider when one reflects on the name of a jealous God.

El-Elyon

El-Elyon: "Most High God." In Genesis 14, Melchizedek, king of Salem, praised Abram's valiant rescue of his nephew Lot.

Blessed be Abram of God Most High [Elyon], possessor of heaven and earth; and blessed be God Most High, who has delivered your enemies into your hand. —Genesis 14:19-20

Melchizedek pointed out to Abram that God delivered his enemies into his hands. Abram gave a tithe of all the war plunder to Melchizedek, as an offering to God. He then gave the remaining ninety percent to the King of Sodom, because he wanted God to receive all the credit for Abram's future success. He wanted his neighbors to realize that Abram served "the Most High God."

Jehovah-Olam

Jehovah-Olam: "The Lord the Everlasting, Uncaused, Eternal, Self-existent One." The book of Genesis says:

> Then Abraham planted a tamarisk tree in Beersheba, and there called on the name of the Lord, the everlasting God.
> —GENESIS 21:33

God has always been, and He will always be. Nothing caused or created God, and nothing will end or finish God. He is eternal. Eternity is a concept that can make our time-constrained heads spin. But for God, it is merely another facet of His name and nature.

Jehovah-Kavod

Jehovah-Kavod: "The Lord of Glory." The Psalms offers a stirring tribute to this name of God:

> Lift up your heads, O you gates! And be lifted up, you everlasting doors. And the King of glory shall come in. Who is this King of glory? The Lord strong and mighty, the Lord mighty in battle. Lift up your heads, O you gates. Lift up, you everlasting doors! And the King of glory shall come in. Who is this King of glory? The Lord of hosts, He is the King of glory. —PSALM 24:7-10

El-Shaddai

El-Shaddai: "The Almighty God; the Double-Breasted God." When God appeared to Abram after the birth of Ishmael, God reminded

Abram of their covenant (Genesis 17:1-3). Despite the obstacles Abram would encounter in his search for the Promised Land, there was no need to become discouraged. Abram simply needed to remember that El-Shaddai would take care of him. Regardless of the situation, Abram had the courage to believe that God would accomplish what He had said He would do. El-Shaddai emphasizes God's ability to handle any situation that confronts His people. God alone is the self-sufficient One.

When we face problems that overwhelm us, we need to remember that El-Shaddai is more powerful than any difficulties we face. If we worship Him, He will fulfill His promises. It is important for us to understand and meditate on the various names of God, because He wants to place His name on our forehead (Revelation 22:4). Inside each of us, God wants to place His complex and rich character, comprising all the glory His names describe.

Jehovah-Tsedek

Jehovah-Tsedek: "The Lord Is Justice." God is a God of justice. He is an unbiased, impartial Judge. "He loves righteousness and justice; the earth is full of the goodness of the Lord," says Psalm 33:5. It's an attribute the prophet Isaiah loved:

> Therefore the Lord will wait, that He may be gracious to you; And therefore He will be exalted, that He may have mercy on you. For the Lord is a God of justice; blessed are all those who wait for Him. —ISAIAH 30:18

Jehovah-Chesed

Jehovah-Chesed: "The Lord Is Merciful." God's mercy overlooks our sin; He is loving, kind, and courteous. His mercy is an aspect of His nature that stirs our hearts. The Psalmists sang repeatedly about the mercy of God: "For the king trusts in the Lord, and through the mercy of the Most High he shall not be moved" (Psalm 21:7). King David sang, "To You, O my Strength, I will sing praises, for God is my defense, my God of mercy" (Psalm 59:17).

The prophets meditated on God's mercy as well. When God showed Himself to Moses, He proclaimed His own goodness to the Israelite:

> The Lord, the Lord God, merciful and gracious, longsuffering, and abounding in goodness and truth, keeping mercy for thousands, forgiving iniquity and transgression and sin, by no means clearing the guilty, visiting the iniquity of the fathers upon the children and the children's children to the third and the fourth generation. —EXODUS 34:6-7

Centuries later, the apostle Paul taught on the compassion of God as well. "Therefore He has mercy on whom He wills, and whom He wills He hardens," he wrote in Romans 9:18.

Jehovah-Magen

Jehovah-Magen: "The Lord a Shield." God loves to protect, hide, and overshadow His children; it's been a commitment of His from the very beginning. As early as in Genesis, God revealed in a vision

His desire to protect Abram (Genesis 15:1): "Do not be afraid, Abram. I am your shield, your exceedingly great reward."

We are a people saved by the Lord (Deuteronomy 33:29), gathered under His wings (Luke 13:34). The safest place in the world to be is in God's care.

Jehovah-Hayah

Jehovah-Hayah: "The Lord is Self-Sufficient, The Great I AM." God holds a unique position in the universe as its only non-created Being. He was, is, and ever more shall be. He is self-creating and self-sustaining.

> Who has ascended into heaven, or descended? Who has gathered the wind in His fists? Who has bound the waters in a garment? Who has established all the ends of the earth? What is His name, and what is His Son's name, if you know? —PROVERBS 30:4

Jehovah-Kadosh

Jehovah-Kadosh: "The Lord Is Holy, Pure, and Undefiled." God stands alone as the source of all purity and holiness. There are beings in Heaven who spend all their time worshipping this aspect of His nature: "Holy, holy, holy is the Lord!" Jesus, by virtue of His Godhood, was also holy, making Him the perfect sacrifice for our sin. In the book of Hebrews it says:

> For such a High Priest was fitting for us who is holy, harmless, undefiled, separate from sinners, and has become higher than the heavens. —HEBREWS 7:26

Our great reward is the ability to praise God's holiness. "Let them praise Your great and awesome name — He is holy," says Psalm 99:3.

Jehovah-Or

Jehovah-Or: "The Lord Is Light." God is light. He is the Luminous One. In Him, there is no darkness at all, metaphorical or literal (1 John 1:5). He is glowing and radiant. "For with You is the fountain of life; In Your light we see light," sang King David in Psalm 36:9.

In Summary

To truly know God's character, we must know His name. When we know His name, we are able to welcome the workings of His character in our own lives. He wants to do this right now wherever we are: at work, in church, in prayer, in meditation, at home, as we sleep. Wherever we are and whatever we are doing, God wants to indelibly imprint His name upon our lives. When we worship God and when we bask in His presence, He loves to place His name upon us.

Are we going to welcome Him? Are we going to become a partner with Him in this process? If we are, then we need to understand His name. We need to hallow it and glorify it as the Name above all names. The closer we draw to Him, the greater the measure of the glory of His names that will be manifested through us.

Our heavenly Father is looking down on earth saying, "I really want to do this for you! I really want to put the fullness of My name on you! I really want to be known for who I am through you! And the way I'm going to be known for who I am is by putting My name, Jehovah-Shalom, on you. Only then will you be at peace! The way I will be known in the world is by putting My name, Jehovah-Rapha, on you so you will be healed. That's how I will be known!"

As you ponder the names of God, you will begin to understand just how great God is. As we come to understand His greatness, we can then call out to Him in our times of need. We must learn to appropriate the power of His name on our behalf in the face of challenging circumstances.

✤ Reflection Questions ✤

1. Have you ever invoked God's name as a refuge from attack?

2. How has He protected you in the past?

3. Has your familiarity with the names of God allowed you to take the benefits of His name for granted? If it has, repent and ask God to give you fresh insight and love for His beautiful names.

4. How has God been righteous in your life?

5. How has God sanctified you?

6. Into what situations that you are facing now would you like God's peace to come?

7. Meditate on the motto, "With God, anywhere. Without God, nowhere." How does it apply to your life?

8. Where would you like to take The Lord Who Heals?

9. What has God provided for you spiritually, physically, emotionally, financially, and mentally?

10. Take a sheet of paper and draw a banner that captures the Lord's role in your life.

11. Find a silent place, close your eyes, and listen for the Good Shepherd's voice. What is He whispering to you today?

12. Can you think of any examples in Scripture of how God predicted the future? Could God speak like this to you?

13. What is the greatest example of God's love that you have ever witnessed?

14. Have you acknowledged God's ownership of your life? How literally should we apply this name to our life?

15. What in your life has become an idol to you? What have you put before God in your world? Are you fully submitted to His will?

16. To whom have you attributed your personal success? Are you waiting for someone to promote you rather than asking God to place that thought in the heart of the one you are looking to?

17. With what kind of perspective does an eternal God view the world around you?

18. How does God view time if He dwells outside of it?

19. Read Psalm 24. Have you completely opened the gates of your heart and life to the King of glory?

20. The Lord receives glory by doing what no one else can do. How has He received glory from your life?

21. What obstacles have you faced as you have searched for your own land of God's promise? How has El-Shaddai helped you?

22. Why was it important that Jesus manifest all the names of God to His followers (John 17:6)?

23. How do God's just ways shine through Psalm 33?

24. Is your life ruled by God's justice?

25. Where has God shown you mercy in your life?

26. Read the words of Jesus in Luke 13:34. How has He gathered you beneath His wing of protection?

27. What does the name "The Self-Sufficient God" mean to you? What does His Son's name mean to you?

28. How does the name of God affect you?

29. Have you read Psalm 99?

30. How has God's light shaped your life?

✦ Recommended Scripture Reading ✦

Psalm 23: The Good Shepherd.

⌐ Make a list of the characteristics of God found in this passage.

⌐ What is the fruit of those who dwell in the Lord's house?

⌐ Which verse especially resonates with your spirit? Why?

chapter *Four*

✤

I Called upon the Name of the Lord

Calling upon the name of the Lord involves taking our knowledge of who He is and applying it to our own lives. If we want to walk in the blessings of His name, we must learn to walk proactively in the authority that His name gives us — authority that must be laid hold of or it will be lost.

Those who bear the name of God become proactive in their language, and with the gaze of their eyes. They become intentional with what they allow out of their mouths and where they allow their eyes to look. If we gain a greater knowledge of who God is by understanding the meaning of His names, then we must apply this knowledge by relying on such truth in the face of trials. We long to carry those names into every situation, risking everything based on His great promises and character. His names become so indelibly stamped on us that we become more like Him in every word and deed.

When our circumstances are pressing in on us, do we fix our gaze upon those problems and speak words of agreement with the anxiety, timidity, and fear that we feel? Or do we fix our eyes on Jesus and proclaim the relevance of His name against our problem? In calling on Jesus, we draw strength and faith from our knowledge of His names, and the beautiful character and promises contained within them. Whatever our need, and whatever our weakness, we can always find our answer and hope in an aspect of His name. Do we need peace? Do we need healing? Do we need deliverance, love, solace, comfort, or direction? They are all contained within His holy name, like an eternal fountain from which every resource flows. When we are tested, we must learn to rely on the truth of His name. Only there will we find our needs met. As the psalmist said:

Then I called upon the name of the Lord: 'O Lord, I implore You, deliver my soul!' Gracious is the Lord, and righteous; Yes, our God is merciful. —PSALM 116:4-5

Psalm 116 is a powerful model of how we can rely on God's name for protection and deliverance. In it, the psalmist talks about several characteristics of God, and the freedom of being able to call upon His name, even in the midst of his darkest hour. "The pains of death surrounded me, and the pangs of Sheol laid hold of me; I found trouble and sorrow," the psalmist sang brokenheartedly. "Then I called upon the name of the Lord: O Lord, I implore You, deliver my soul!" The author then reminded God of the majesty contained within His name: "Gracious is the Lord, and righteous; Yes, our God is merciful. The Lord preserves the simple; I was brought low, and He saved me."

Thousands of years later, we still have that same ability to call on the name of the Lord. This is part of our heritage as Christians, a portion of the inheritance left to us by God the Father and Jesus His Son. Our primary responsibility, the psalmist explained, is to accept and honor the freedom God brings us: "What shall I render to the Lord for all His benefits toward me? I will take up the cup of salvation, and call upon the name of the Lord."

Finally, the psalmist sang, when God does deliver us, we have one final duty: thankfulness. "O Lord, truly I am Your servant; I am Your servant, the son of Your maidservant; You have loosed my bonds," he wrote. "I will offer to You the sacrifice of thanksgiving, and will call upon the name of the Lord."

This simple three-step model, as revealed in Psalm 116, is a good starting point for incorporating the names of God into our lives. First, we must remind God of His names and worship Him for them. Second, we must accept the freedom and blessing those names entail. Third, we must be thankful for the glory He reveals to us in His names. The final step to incorporating the names of God into our lives is to make a conscious effort to apply His names to our every aspect and decision.

The Inheritance of the Father

When one is named, he or she is made an heir to the resources and wealth of whoever named them. Likewise, Colossians 2:9 says that we have been given fullness in Christ. In other words, we lack nothing when we place our complete faith in Him. When Jesus was crucified, we became marked with His blood, much like the ancient

Israelites' doorposts were marked during the slaughter of the Egyptians' firstborn sons during Moses' time. God's name, through Jesus' blood, has been put on us, identifying us as being under His protection and sovereignty. Under that care, we have been given all of the resources of God's names.

It would be tragic if we failed to seize our full inheritance in Jesus' name. Yet, millions of God's children, through the ages, have missed out on the full measure of His resources simply because of their misunderstanding of the nature of God. Many, though sons and daughters of a glorious King, still live as paupers. Heaven forbid, we squander our inheritance! We must rely on God's provision in our lives. The only reason we are able to be proactive in our faith is because God has already given us an open door to the warehouse of His resources. When He placed His name on us, He also placed His promise in us, that like a Shepherd and King, He would care for our every need.

The Desperate Heart

Only the desperate heart is faithful and quick to call upon the name of the Lord. God responds to prayers of desperation, because desperation is an attitude that helps preserve sincerity of faith. The desperate heart has seen the truth and has abandoned all to lay hold of it; it knows that its hope is found nowhere else but in God. The psalmist was desperate for God to save him in Psalm 116, and God did, through the power of His name. A lack of desperation leaves the heart unfocused, and living in such a comfort zone creates an attitude of distraction and self-sufficiency. Ultimately, that distracted heart can fall into deception because it has chosen to stray from the truth it first saw when it opened up to Jesus. Truly desperate people don't have time to be distracted because they know their situation is of life-and-death importance.

My friend Paul Cain once said, "If God is not speaking to you as He used to, go back and do the things you used to do." Do we really know that He is all we need? Have we yet snapped out of the illusion that we have control over our lives? Have we realized that Jesus is absolutely necessary for our survival? Or do we still think we can make it on our own?

Satan, the king of lies, loves to create illusions that keep us bound by chains of deception. These are false paradigms that prevent us from calling out in radical desperation, "Come, save me, O God! Come and deliver me!" Such cries are full of faith, made by people who have learned to call on the name of the Lord with all their heart.

Taking Hold of His Name

Those who want God to place His name on them must reach out and take hold of the promise they have been given. In other words, they must "call upon the name of the Lord," as the psalmist did in Psalm 116.

As we learn to call on the name of the Lord, He will not only bring us outward deliverance but He will change us on the inside. He begins to work the character of His name into the very fiber of our being, intermingling His Holy Spirit with our own spirit. This process of change is difficult and painful, but absolutely necessary to walking fully in the promise and shelter of God's name.

✤ Reflection Questions ✤

1. What kind of trials are you facing at the moment?

2. What facet of God's name is He wanting to teach you by allowing you to go through this trial?

3. What aspect of God's name would help you in the trial you currently face? Pray and ask God to give you that name.

4. Using the Psalm 116 model, how can you apply a name of God to a situation you currently face? Pray and worship God for His majesty, accept the blessing that comes with His holy name, and thank Him for His mercy.

5. When was the last time you felt desperate spiritually?

6. What happened?

✤ Recommended Scripture Reading ✤

Psalm 116: A Cry of Desperation.

⌐ Make a list of the characteristics of God found in this passage.

⌐ What do you suppose the psalmist was facing that led him to this desperate place?

⌐ Which verse especially resonates with your spirit? Why?

✠

chapter Five

Blessed Are All Those Who Wait for Him

God is looking far and wide for those He can trust to bear His name, who won't be corrupted by the blessings it will bring. He loves us too much to give His name to us before we are ready, because He knows we will be tempted to abuse it, and He will be forced to pour out His judgment on us. God loves us too much to put us in a situation that is more than we can handle, as Paul explained:

> No temptation has overtaken you except such as is common to man; but God is faithful, who will not allow you to be tempted beyond what you are able, but with the

temptation will also make the way of escape, that you may be able to bear it. —1 CORINTHIANS 10:13

The Bible makes it clear that all flesh will be judged for how it uses God's name (Exodus 20:7; Matthew 5:34). Therefore, God will not give us His name when He knows He will have to judge us harshly for it later. He will reserve His name and the blessings it brings for those with the character and humility to carry it properly. As the prophet Isaiah said:

Therefore the Lord will wait, that He may be gracious to you; and therefore He will be exalted, that He may have mercy on you. For the Lord is a God of justice; blessed are all those who wait for Him. —ISAIAH 30:18

God will wait to release His blessing and glory until our character is ready to carry His name in integrity.

Many people eagerly seek the blessings of having God's name placed upon them, but they are not ready for the temptations and challenges that will accompany such a gift. We need to hold ourselves accountable: Are we truly ready for the adulation that ensues because of the blessings of His name? Are we ready for all the people who will line up at our doors for prayer? Are we ready for the incredible spiritual attack that will come against us, causing us to become proud and to believe that our blessings have something to do with us? We must ask ourselves these difficult questions before we seek the imprint of God's name on our lives, otherwise we will bring His judgment on ourselves.

Embracing the Fire of Testing

To carry God's name, we must choose to put on the robe of His character and the cloak of humility, and vow not to wear any other covering no matter how comfortable it may seem. God wants to teach us how to die to our own cares so that we might be free to live for His glory and the good of others.

We are called by God to give ourselves completely to the working of His ways within us. This requires us to rid ourselves of any and all markings of our flesh nature, even the ones we have been unwilling to let go of until this point. Our motto must be the same as the apostle Paul's: "More of Him and less of me!"

How do we completely rid ourselves of our selfish ways? We can't, but He can. God does so through the purging work of His holy fire. In the same way that heat causes the infection in a wound to be drawn to the surface, so too will God use fiery circumstances to bring the sin in our lives to the surface. He wants us to deal with the things that hold us back from a renewed, healthy relationship with Him.

Most of the time we have the luxury of avoiding heated circumstances; we have learned to manipulate and compromise our way through life so that we escape the unpleasant fire of testing.

But, to have God's name placed on us, we must trust Him with the work of His fire. We must trust Him when He allows trying and despairing times to appear. If we do not turn aside, God will use that fire to help us discover all manner of evil rising from our souls. He does this so He can boil it off and forever cleanse it away.

We can do ourselves a tremendous favor when we give up denying the seriousness of our sinful state, and become truly serious about the remedy of God's ability to purify us and keep us holy, accomplished through the blood of His Son and the confession of our sins. Will we run or will we trust? That is the test before us.

Learning the Posture of Spiritual Brokenness

Passing this test means we have become broken before God, completely reliant on His power and grace to survive. The spiritually broken one has finally rejected the lie that says we are whole, or that we can heal ourselves. Only those who walk in brokenness will be clean enough to be marked by God's name.

Our lives are spent trying to rationalize our sin away. We give ourselves constant pep talks to try and overcome our sin: If we would just work harder, or study more, or practice longer, or save more money or find a different church, then we could overcome our issues. These are the futile hopes of people who have yet to embrace the humble posture of spiritual brokenness. To be branded with God's names, we must admit the reality of our human condition.

Spiritually broken people exchange their weaknesses for the strengths of God. They live in the same hope that God gave the apostle Paul:

> My grace is sufficient for you, for My strength is made perfect in weakness. —2 CORINTHIANS 12:9

Rather than denying the presence of doubt, it is admitted, confessed, and then exchanged for the supernatural gift of faith. Rather than denying the presence of fear, it is admitted, confessed, and then exchanged for the supernatural gift of courage. Anxiety is exchanged for hope, hatred is exchanged for love, weakness is exchanged for strength, and any other need is fully admitted and then fully exchanged. Our brokenness, our confession that we are weak, becomes the currency needed to buy the strength and freedom God's name brings.

Surrender to God is not a negative, defeatist attitude; rather, it is the most positive worldview one can have. Hands are finally released from the frenzy of trying to make life work and instead are raised to Heaven with the cries of desperate prayers. God truly wants to be our "all-in-all." We are given the freedom simply to be God's children and saved from the feeling that we must earn that authority. Broken people know that God alone is their help. Even more than that, He is their very life. They live as Paul did:

> Therefore I take pleasure in infirmities, in reproaches, in needs, in persecutions, in distresses, for Christ's sake. For when I am weak, then I am strong. —2 CORINTHIANS 12:10

Obedience and Submission

God is looking for a people who are not merely obedient, but obedient and submissive. I began pondering this distinction in my own spiritual walk after the Lord spoke to me and said, "Son, you're obedient, but you're not submissive."

"Lord, what are You talking about?" I replied.

He said, "You obey Me, but when you do, you're like the little boy who sat down and told his mom, 'I may be sitting down on the outside, but I'm standing up on the inside.' You may be obedient, but you are not submissive."

Suddenly I felt my heart being exposed.

He went on to say, "Son, I want a submissive people. I want you to be submissive to My will . . . not merely obedient to My will. True obedience grows out of submission. You'll do what I ask, but you argue the whole time you are doing it. You say things like, 'I wish I didn't have to do this. Why is God asking me to do this? Why couldn't He have chosen somebody else? I don't want to go there; I don't like that kind of food.'"

Many people think that obedience to God automatically releases His blessings. However, obedience without a heart of submission will actually serve to hinder the blessings of God in our lives. We must be completely submitted to His will. Scripture tells us that God desires obedience more than sacrifice. Why? Because obedience is the sacrifice of our own goals for another's goals. Thus, obedience is a greater sacrifice. Submission, as the highest level of obedience, is an even greater sacrifice.

The Longing Heart of God Urging Us On

God longs to place His names on us — every one of them! God delights in seeing us carry His name in a way that helps to make Him known for who He really is. How do we rightly carry His name? By holding it in the highest regard in our hearts, by hallowing it. We must esteem, admire, honor, respect, praise, and cherish the unspeakable treasure of His glory. This is how we are to carry God's name; this is how we hallow it in our hearts.

God wants to reveal His greatness through us. Scripture says,

> For the Lord will not forsake His people, for His great name's sake, because it has pleased the Lord to make you His people. —1 SAMUEL 12:22

God is not up in Heaven saying, "Okay, since I said I would forgive you, I'll forgive you because I have to. I'll forgive you, but I'm not going to use you."

This is not what God wants to do. He does not want to withhold from us the privilege of service to Him. God is pleased to make us His people, and this means being a people marked by His name.

Overcoming Our Excuses

We live in an exciting and profound season, for God is calling us into our destiny. He is calling us to boldly bear His name by walking out His character in the daily routine and mundane reality of our lives. C. S. Lewis wrote, "We are half-hearted creatures, fooling about with drink and sex and ambition when infinite joy is offered us, like an ignorant child who wants to go on making mud pies in a slum because he cannot imagine what is meant by the offer of a holiday at the sea." There are too many mud pies lying around.

Sadly, in the face of such an invitation, many of us may still say things like, "But I'm so weak." We may even whine a little, and then say, "But I'm in a spiritual hospital bed and I am being fed intravenously right now . . . I've been this way for the last twenty-five years." Or we may think up any number of other excuses to avoid the submission it takes to fully carry the blessing and authority of God's name. We settle for mediocrity, for being lukewarm.

To all of us, God says, "You are the perfect candidate, because in your weakness I will be shown strong."

I have noticed something in Scripture: anytime God wants to do something truly remarkable, He looks for the weakest person He can find to do it. A perfect example of this principle is the life of Gideon.

Gideon received a powerful angelic visitation, as God called him to lead the Israelites to victory (Judges 6). Gideon was unmoved by God's faith in him. Instead, he answered: "God, do you have any clue who I am? Don't You know I'm from the tribe of Manasseh? Don't You know that the tribe of Manasseh is the weakest tribe in all of Israel? And not only that, my family is the weakest clan in the tribe of Manasseh. Even more, I'm the weakest in all my family! So You have got to be kidding!"

I can almost hear the Angel of the Lord chuckle as he answered, "Yes, Gideon . . . God has looked all over for you."

We need to know that God is not afraid of our weakness. He wants us to get out of our spiritual hospital beds, rip the intravenous tubes out of our arms, and boldly declare, "Here I am, Lord! Send me!"

Tom's Escape from Death

God still loves to use the most unlikely people to change the world. Tom Washington works twelve stories underground in Birmingham, England. He's one of the very few oncologists — doctors who study and treat cancerous and other tumors — whom the World Health Organization listens to. However, his life has not always looked as successful as it does today.

Tom grew up in Uganda during the genocidal reign of Idi Amin. Amin, a brutal dictator, killed 300,000 Ugandans in the last half of the twentieth century. When he was just a boy, Tom was forced to stand in a firing line while his entire village was machine-gunned by Amin's men. Everyone to the right and left of Tom died, but amazingly he was missed. Tom fell to the ground with the others, as his father and his uncle fell on top of him. He was trapped under their bodies. While lying on the ground, he escaped the notice of the soldiers. When they left, he got up and fled for safety.

On two other occasions, while Tom was riding in a bus, someone threw a hand grenade inside. In both incidents, everyone was killed but him.

Many years later, Tom went to medical school, climbing to the top of his class. One day while walking with his best friend from Uganda on the streets of London, England, a sudden and bizarre occurrence took place: Tom's heart burst open — it literally tore itself nearly in half.

Amazingly, his friend recognized what was going on as Tom collapsed to the sidewalk. He reached into his pocket and took out a pocketknife and slit open Tom's side. He stuck his hand between Tom's ribs and squeezed his heart in order to make it beat.

The ambulance finally arrived and took Tom to the hospital. Tom's friend was continuing to squeeze the heart, while at the same time screaming at Tom not to die. They put Tom on the operating table, and after doing all they could, they sadly knew he was going to die within forty-eight hours.

While lying in the recovery room, Tom awoke to see many tubes going in and out of him. He recognized the color of the blood going through the tubes and, based upon his medical school training, knew he was being artificially kept alive. He also knew that he did not have long to live.

As he was looking at all these tubes going into his chest, nose, and mouth, he suddenly felt a presence in the room. When he looked across the room, he saw the Lord standing there. Jesus said to him, "Tom, I'm going to heal you. Get up and go home." The Lord walked over to him, put His hand on Tom's chest, and said, "You're healed, Tom." Then He disappeared.

Tom looked at the tubes, and the color of the blood was still the same. Nothing had changed, but Tom faced the test of his life. Who did he believe: Jehovah-Rapha, The Lord Who Heals, or his own medical school training? Deciding to trust the Lord's words more than what he was seeing, he said, "Well, the Lord said I'm healed, so I'm healed!" He pulled all of the tubes and everything else out of his chest, mouth and nose, got up, and went to the nurses' station.

"Where are my clothes?" Tom asked the stunned nurses. "I'm going home. The Lord has healed me."

Hospital workers didn't want to let him go, so Tom said, "Okay. I'll leave and walk home in my gown. The Lord told me I was healed, and He said to go home. So whether you help me or not, I am going home." The next morning Tom was at the local YMCA, swimming. Today, Tom is on the verge of an incredible immunological discovery, and he's doing clinical trials in his native Uganda.

God is seeking obedience, submission, and weakness to make strong. It is people like Tom Washington on whom God is looking to put His name. He is looking for people who will be fully submitted to Him even in the face of "impossibilities." God wants to put His name on us, but He doesn't want to put it on us in the same way that we carry the name Christian or the way we may bear our family's name. Instead, He wants to brand us with His name and bind us to His purposes with a faith that won't waver or die.

God Is Staking His Name on Us

God's great mercy toward us is founded upon His name. He longs to bond with us and make us one with Him. The apostle Paul wrote:

He who is joined to the Lord is one spirit with Him.
—1 CORINTHIANS 6:17.

Becoming one with the Lord is just the beginning. Those who are one in Spirit with the Lord are called to take on His attributes, and this means taking on His name. This goes far beyond merely being called a Christian.

I love the words of author John Piper: "It was God's good pleasure to join you to Himself in such a way that His name is at stake in your destiny." Imagine that: God longs to join Himself to you in such a way that His name is at stake in you!

That is exactly what God has done. When we were rescued from the realm of darkness and brought into the Kingdom of Light, He said, "Welcome. You are called by My name, and I am going to put that name on you. It doesn't matter what you think about yourself; I know where you're going and I know why I created you. I love you more than anything else. I am not only going to put My name on you, but I'm going to prepare you to bear it. Why? Because I will not put anything on you that is greater than what you can bear. You will feel like you can't handle it, but you will, because I will prepare you and enable you to carry it. You will carry My name to the world."

As we learn to embrace God's work of preparation in our lives, we will soon begin to reap the blessings of bearing His name. No matter what the cost we pay in the work of preparation, it will never compare with the unspeakable blessings we will gain from being marked by His name.

❖ Reflection Questions ❖

1. Have you ever truly been tempted beyond what you thought that you could bear?

2. Why does God make us this promise in 1 Corinthians 10:13?

3. What challenges do people who carry the name of God face?

4. Is your character ready for those challenges?

5. Is there a sin in your life that you have been denying the seriousness of?

6. How does God view that issue?

7. Would you like to be free from it? Pray and ask God for forgiveness and to wipe your slate clean.

8. What will you *not* receive, if sin is not dealt with in your life?

9. Is there a weakness in your life you would like to exchange for God's strength? How might your life be different if you were to allow this to happen?

10. Has there been a situation in your life where you have been obedient but not submissive?

11. What was God's highest plan for that situation? Did that actually occur? How do you know?

12. What stirred in your spirit when you read Tom's story?

13. Would you take Jehovah-Rapha at His word if you were in Tom's situation? Why?

❖ Recommended Scripture Reading ❖

Judges 6-8: Gideon Delivers Israel.

⌒ How did God prepare Gideon to lead His people?

⌒ What do the prophetic signs in this passage tell us about the nature of God?

⌒ Which verse especially resonates with your spirit? Why?

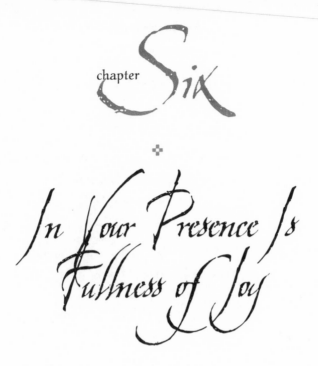

✢

chapter Six

In Your Presence Is Fullness of Joy

Of all the blessings found in bearing God's name, one stands above the rest: salvation. This is the very core of what Jesus Christ has accomplished for those who carry His name. As it says in the book of Acts:

> There is salvation in no one else for there is no other name under heaven, given men by which we must be saved. —ACTS 4:12, NASB

Without Jesus, we were lost and without hope. Still, out of His tremendous love, He has given us His name and the fullness of hope that comes with it.

Salvation is not merely the eternal life we enter into when we die. Rather, it is a quality of life we can begin to experience now, a life filled with His presence. As King David sang in Psalm 16:11, "You will show me the path of life; in Your presence is fullness of joy; at Your right hand are pleasures forevermore."

The presence of the Lord releases His saving power — power to dispel hopelessness, power to bring healing, power to defeat fear, and power to overcome the effect of sin in our lives. This is what it means to walk in the saving power of God, and this is the blessing that awaits those who bear His name.

God's Glory

In speaking to Jeremiah, God says:

> For as the sash clings to the waist of a man, so I have caused the whole house of Israel and the whole house of Judah to cling to Me, says the Lord; that they may become My people . . . —JEREMIAH 13:11

God wants us to become His people for His renown. As we learn how to bear His name, we then become respected and honored among people, and this causes God's name to grow in renown. As He allows us to experience His mighty acts and we give Him the honor for it, our lives give Him glory.

When we learn to cling to the Lord, we become a vehicle that brings Him great honor. Clinging to Him takes passion and faithful devotion. Those who cling to the Lord are those who love to praise and worship Him. Isaiah understood this principle: He declared that we were all created to give God praise (Isaiah 43:21).

In the book of Romans, we again see that God created us for the purpose of bringing glory to His name:

> For the Scripture says to the Pharaoh, "For this very purpose I've raised you up, that I may show My power in you, and that My name may be declared in all the earth."
> —ROMANS 9:17

God wants to pour His glory through us, as long as our hearts are humble and faithful. Those cloaked in humility are the ones God will entrust with His glorious splendor. He hungers for this so that His greatness will be displayed to the world, and so that more people will be freed from their imprisonment in the kingdom of darkness.

Victory and Power

My ministry was recently given ninety acres of land atop a high hill in New Hampshire. The stone walls surrounding this hill were built in 1746, and for the past two centuries, the peak has been used as an altar of Satan. Every time I go there, I have to tear down the many occultic altars that have been built. I break them into pieces, but each time I return, new ones have been put up. Satanists rebuild the altars by hauling in new rock that isn't native to the hill. We are literally taking back a high place.

God is calling us to take back the "high places" of idolatry, witchcraft, and sin as well. He wants us to move beyond "doing church" and actually begin to live as the Church. The Lord wants us to take back the enemy's land that belongs to God. God wants to begin taking us into the arenas we have been prepared for, but this means we will have to become strong in Him.

To do this, God needs to put His name on us. He longs for us to know — to truly understand — that His name is the most powerful name on the face of the earth. He wants to make a glorious name for Himself in us and through us. When He touches down in our lives, people will say, "There's no way he or she could have done that. It must have been God."

Those who are marked by the name of the Lord have been given an open window to Heaven's authority. God wants to place on us the very same name that routed the ancient armies of Old Testament times through His servants Moses, Joshua, Gideon, David, and the other heroes of the faith. This is the same name that released the deadly plagues against Egypt, and then split open the Red Sea. It brought water in the desert and food from Heaven. It tore down the walls of Jericho and slew the giant Goliath.

It was by this same name that the early Church in the book of Acts performed mighty signs and wonders to verify the message of the Gospel. It is this name that raised Christ from the dead! It is this blessed name that God is offering us today! Receive His name, and receive the blessings He longs to pour out in your life.

Rahab's Testimony: Godly Reputation

When Rahab was talking to the Israeli spies in her house, she said,

> We have heard how the Lord dried up the water of the Red Sea for you when you came out of Egypt, and what you did to the two kings of the Amorites who were on the other side of the Jordan, Sihon and Og, whom you utterly destroyed. And as soon as we heard these things, our hearts melted; neither did there remain any more courage in anyone because of you, for the Lord your God, He is God in heaven above and on earth beneath. —Joshua 2:10-11

When you walked into a corporate meeting, have you ever heard someone say, "We've heard of you! We heard how you slew the companies that stood in your way, for the God of Heaven and earth is with you?"

When you entered a city council meeting, have you heard people say, "We've heard of what you did, and our hearts melted?"

When you walked into a prayer meeting in your church, did the ground quake and people say, "We've heard how God answers your prayers, how He has destroyed the evil surrounding you and how He set your family free?"

That is the kind of people God is looking for — people who will bear His name. He's not looking for the noble, He's not looking for the wise, and He's not looking for the strong. He is simply looking for those who will hallow His name. He wants the weakest of the weak, as Gideon was.

Those who are marked by the name of the Lord will experience increased favor in their reputation. Look at the life of Joseph the dreamer. Joseph was a man who constantly found favor in the most difficult of situations. As a lowly slave in Potiphar's house, he was inexplicably given favor and put in charge of the entire estate:

> And his master saw that the Lord was with him and that the Lord made all he did to prosper in his hand. So Joseph found favor in his sight, and served him. Then he made him overseer of his house, and all that he had he put under his authority. —GENESIS 39:3-4

In prison a few years later, Joseph soon found himself in authority over all the other prisoners: "But the Lord was with Joseph and showed him mercy, and He gave him favor in the sight of the keeper of the prison" (Genesis 39:21).

After that, Pharaoh himself plucked Joseph from the jail and made him the second-in-command of all Egypt:

> Then Pharaoh said to Joseph, "Inasmuch as God has shown you all this, there is no one as discerning and wise as you. You shall be over my house, and all my people shall be ruled according to your word; only in regard to the throne will I be greater than you." —GENESIS 41:39-40

Now that's favor!

Favor from the Lord comes because His name carries it. Joseph was branded by God, and God's favor rested on his life. Others will take note of the blessing and authority of the Lord manifested in the lives of those who humbly carry His name, and, as a result, people's attention will be drawn to God.

A Willing Vessel with Childlike Faith

God made this truth incredibly clear to me one night as I was ministering in a church near San Diego, California. God's power was moving wonderfully. Prayer lines were filled at the front of the church. A little boy named Daniel, only four or five years old, walked up to me on the platform. Daniel had Down's syndrome. He walked up to me, grabbed my leg, and began to hug it. I tousled his hair. Then he let go and walked over to the worship team and pretended that he was strumming a guitar and playing the drums. He was having a wonderful time.

As I watched Daniel, I was also praying and asking the Holy Spirit to help me understand His plans for the night. Shortly I would understand in a way I had never anticipated. Daniel made his rounds and returned to grab my leg again. This time, Daniel squeezed it . . . really tight. Once again, I began to rumple his hair, and as I was doing this he looked up at me with an incredibly huge grin. I then heard the Lord speak to me. He said, "Pick this boy up. I want to show him what I'm doing."

Joyfully I picked him up, thinking, "Well, he is so short, he just can't see over the people ministering down front. If I pick him up, then he'll be able to see what's happening." Many people were already laid out on the floor, being ministered to by the Holy Spirit. So I picked Daniel up in my arms, and as I was looking at him, he smiled, and then suddenly a pastor's greatest fear occurred. Daniel grabbed the microphone out of my hand.

Immediately he began to point at people and speak powerful words of healing over them. He would point into the crowd saying, "Lady, lady, come and receive more power!" He would then declare, "More power!" Then, boom! Down she fell. Then he pointed to another person, "Man, man, white shirt, more power! More power!" And again, boom! Down he went.

Daniel called out a dozen people just like that, maybe even more. By now I was a tearful mess and was praying, "Now I understand what You wanted. Father, You were showing him what You were doing. And when he saw what You were doing, he decided he wanted to do it too."

Then the Lord said to me, "Son, I don't need intelligent men. I don't need tall men. I don't need short men. I don't need thin men. I don't need heavy men. I don't need people who are good-looking. All I need is a willing vessel."

Daniel's parents later told me Daniel had never spoken a word until that evening. God took a child who couldn't even speak and used him to heal many people, and melt my heart.

The weaker we are, the greater His glory will be manifested. God is simply looking for willing vessels in which He can dwell. As the apostle Paul wrote:

> He said to me, "My grace is sufficient for you, for My strength is made perfect in weakness." Therefore most gladly I will rather boast in my infirmities, that the power of Christ may rest upon me . . . For when I am weak, then I am strong. —2 CORINTHIANS 12:9-10

❖ Reflection Questions ❖

1. Have you ever experienced the fullness of God's joy?

2. What was that experience like?

3. When you look at your life before and after meeting Christ, how has it changed?

4. Has anyone seen God's greatness displayed in your life? When?

5. What is the difference between "doing church" and living as the Church?

6. In your life, which have you been doing?

7. Is there a special arena God has been preparing to take you?

8. Have you received God's name?

9. Would you like to carry the Lord's favor?

10. What could that look like in your life? Dream big!

11. Ask the Lord to come and pour out His favor on you today.

❖ Recommended Scripture Reading ❖

Genesis 37, 39-41: Joseph the Dreamer.

How did God prepare Joseph to carry His name and favor?

In what ways did Joseph manifest the names of God?

Which verse especially resonates with your spirit? Why?

chapter *Seven*

✤

Holy unto the Lord

Some boast in chariots, and some in horses; but we will boast in the name of the Lord, our God. —PSALM 20:7, NASB

In the same way that the Levite priests of the Old Testament bore the words "Holy unto the Lord" on their foreheads, we, too, must bear the holy name of the Lord in our lives. For such a marking to occur, we must understand what it will cost. We must get a glimpse of what such a marked life will look like.

The Mark of Consecration

God is calling us to be a people marked by His name, to become willing vessels who have removed any unconsecrated things from our lives and any unholy affections from our hearts.

We will be stretched and have to deal with new issues that He reveals to us as we grow in Him. While our friends are getting away with certain behaviors, God will call us to a higher standard of holiness and morality. All of those old, lesser things will need to fall by the wayside, because His name needs to become dearer to us than anything else.

In order for God to create the necessary consecration in our lives, He will have to help us in submitting different levels of our lives to Him. Some of these areas are:

❖ *Affections.* God wants to align our heart more perfectly with His. He desires for us to shed any affection that might steal the focus of our heart away from Him. The Bible speaks of the Church as the Bride of Christ. Every bride is given the name of her husband. So too we have been given the name of Jesus. Through His blood we have been made one with Him, as in the mystery of marriage, and our affections should reflect that love.

❖ *Thoughts.* A life that is marked by the name of the Lord is a life consecrated at the level of thinking. This life has learned to focus its thoughts on whatever is pure, right, holy, and good (Philippians 4:8) rather than on any of the cares and concerns of this world — which is always where the world pushes us to focus.

❖ *Actions.* Those who are marked by the name of the Lord experience a purging of activities in their lives; many things are cut away — things that may have been good but not spiritually profitable or fruit-producing. God will free us from the distractions and entanglements that have kept us from fully pursuing him. Those with the mark of consecration regularly ask themselves questions such as: "Why am I doing this?" "Is this activity glorifying God, or is it just satisfying a craving of my flesh?" "Is this activity stealing my time from something else God is already calling me to do?" God is calling us to be much more discriminating about the activities we give ourselves to — we can no longer afford to waste our energy on pursuits that don't really matter and are not truly profitable.

❖ **Time.** How do we use our time? Do we lavish it on ourselves, or do we lavish it on others through the service of our lives and resources? A life marked by the name of the Lord does not grasp onto time as though it were its own. Stewardship of time, too, has been consecrated to the Lord. The Sabbath, a period of rest, is observed in the life of such a believer because it is a weekly reminder that our life is not our own and that all we have is truly His.

❖ **Finances.** Our finances are an investment into the passions of our life. The life marked by the name of the Lord is truly humble and servantlike. It does not spend its money on itself but freely invests it in others. This lifestyle understands the words of Jesus: "It is more blessed to give than to receive" (Acts 20:35). This life depicts godly wisdom and understanding that finances advance the Kingdom of God. This is a life that not only understands but implements the law of the harvest, and is not bound by a spirit of poverty.

God is not merely looking for people who are obedient, but rather He is seeking people who are submissive to His will. God is looking for willing vessels upon whom He can trust to put His name.

The Mark of His Presence

> But you shall seek the place where the Lord your God chooses, out of all your tribes, to put His name for His dwelling place . . . —DEUTERONOMY 12:5

My friend Bob Jones once said, "Where God puts His name, His presence abides." When God puts His name on us, His presence will live with us continually. We won't merely visit His presence, but His presence will remain in us. Where we go, He will go.

There are many ways of telling if a person has been marked by the presence of God:

❖ **Joy.** In the presence of the Lord there is fullness of joy (Psalm 16:11).

❖ **Peace.** Those marked by the name of the Lord will be set free from anxieties and fears; they will instead be governed by peace (John 14:27).

❖ **Love.** God is love (1 John 4:16). Jesus also tells us that love is the distinguishing witness upon us to unbelievers.

❖ **Light.** Jesus says that in Him we are made the light of the world (Matthew 5:14).

❖ **Hope.** Those who are marked by the name of the Lord bear the hope of His presence. They know that nothing else is secure (Romans 5:1-2).

❖ **Healing.** Those who are marked by the presence of the Lord will discover Him as the One who heals all our sickness (Exodus 15:26). God's presence always results in healing: spirit, soul, and/or body.

❖ *Fruit of the Spirit.* Paul wrote in Galatians 5:22-23 that true believers bear the fruit of the Holy Spirit: love, joy, peace, long suffering, kindness, goodness, faithfulness, gentleness, and self-control. God's presence in our lives will produce this fruit.

There are many other descriptions we could list of those who are marked by the presence of the Lord. It is safe to say that those who are branded by the name of the Lord will manifest an amazing quality of life — a life filled with the presence of God. They will produce great fruit of the Spirit, as listed in Galatians 5:22-23. Most likely, it will not happen instantly, as there are too many hidden issues we are blind to; but if we do not give up, this life in God can be ours.

The Mark of Authority

Authority can be inherited along the lines of a name because a person's name includes the authority associated with that person's position and place. For example, we may hear such things as, "In the name of the law . . ." or, "In the name of the king . . ." or, more importantly, we may have used the phrase "In the name of Jesus." Those phrases can only be used effectively by people who have been delegated authority under the law or by Jesus Himself. If we are marked by the name of the Lord, we will bear the authority intrinsic to His presence.

This, however, brings up an issue with the use of the Lord's name. Often we have heard people passionately praying for things from God. They fervently pray and at the end of uttering all their requests, they simply say, "In the name of Jesus." The unfortunate thing is that sometimes such zealous ones do not maintain a lifestyle that reflects the character of Christ. They have inadvertently reduced the Lord's name to a kind of lucky rabbit's foot.

The life of the believer, when it reflects the character of Jesus, is the life that is able to lay hold of the authority of God. The source of authority is not merely in the name itself but in the character represented by the name. If we are marked by the name of the Lord, then we will also be marked by the character and therefore the authority of Jesus.

The Mark of Humility and Brokenness

The apostle James wrote that God resists the proud but gives grace to the humble (Proverbs 3:34; James 4:6). Jesus was the ultimate servant; the gospels say that He was meek and lowly of heart.

Those who are marked by the name of God are those who have embraced the value of humility and have discovered the mystery of God's grace. Grace speaks of the supernatural endowment of God to help us be what we are not and to do what we cannot. Those who are humble shall be great in the Kingdom because they have learned to keep themselves within the scope of God's work. They have learned to deny themselves in order to serve Christ more fully. Jesus Himself spoke of the value of the humble in His Sermon on the Mount: "Blessed are the poor in spirit, for theirs is the kingdom of heaven" (Matthew 5:3).

One of the greatest dangers in the Kingdom of God is the sin of spiritual pride. Those who wear the mark of humility find a potent shield of protection against this vice. These people no longer worry about having to prove anything to anyone — they are totally secure in the Father's love and acceptance. They bear the mark of humility because they bear the name of God.

Unfortunately, through frequent and common use, the word *humility* has become stripped of its meaning.

Christian musician Steve Fry has compiled many of the qualities that display humility:

❖ **Correctable.** The spiritually broken person is easily correctable and actively seeks correction from those they trust.

❖ **Identity.** The spiritually broken person doesn't derive his or her identity from what he or she does but has relinquished all needs for affirmation over to the Lord. This is what the apostle Paul meant when he wrote that "he made Himself of no reputation" (Philippians 2:7).

❖ **Freedom.** Spiritually broken people are free from having to establish their self-worth; they are not defensive nor seeking to justify themselves. They know spiritual boundaries, which brings security and freedom in the Kingdom of God.

❖ **Servant.** Spiritually broken people look for opportunities to serve other people's interests and regularly choose the path of least personal interest. They are not driven by opportunities but have reconciled themselves to obscurity. They have relinquished the expectation of prominence or greatness.

❖ **Forgiving.** The spiritually broken person is not afraid to admit he or she is wrong but is quick to ask for forgiveness and to forgive others who have hurt him or her. Forgiving others is often more difficult than asking to be forgiven.

Why is it important to list these components of a life marked by the name of the Lord? Because God's names are at stake in us. People will see God through the manifestation of His names in our lifestyles.

Conclusion

What an amazing God we serve! How could anyone ever want anything more than the gift of His name? Remember what King David sang:

> Some boast in chariots, and some in horses; but we will boast in the name of the Lord, our God. —PSALM 20:7, NASB

In Hebrew, the phrase *to boast in* means "to have confidence in, to trust in." Boasting in God's name indicates that we have confidence in His character, His attributes, His nature — who He is. God longs to free us from our sinful tendencies of doubt and self-promotion and our habit of trying to draw our confidence from our own resources or those of the people around us. This is the way of the world. But God's way is different.

There is a level of confidence and assurance that God offers us far surpassing any confidence the world could ever know. The confidence of the world can be shaken because ultimately it is dependent upon human strength. The confidence God wants to give is never-ending; it cannot be disappointed, it cannot falter, it cannot fail because it is rooted in the very foundation of His sovereign presence, character, and nature. It is rooted in the unshakable foundation of His hallowed name!

God is extending the fullness of His name to you today. He is offering to put His name on you and give you every blessing that comes with it. How will you respond? Are you ready for the fire of preparation necessary for all who desire to receive His name? As you embark on this adventure of knowing God, let Him show you the amazing mystery and wonder reserved for those who have chosen to receive and bear His name. It truly is the name above all names.

❖ Reflection Questions ❖

1. Where do your affections lie?

2. Are there any sinful affections you need to repent of?

3. What consumes your thoughts?

4. Are there any sinful thoughts you need to repent of?

5. Why do you do what you do?

6. Do your actions glorify God, or satisfy your own personal desires?

7. Are there any sinful actions you need to repent of?

8. Do you do things that steal your time away from God?

9. What do you lavish your time on?

10. Do you need to repent for the way you spend your time?

11. Do you spend too much money on ungodly priorities?

12. How much do you give God? How much do you give the poor?

13. Do you need to repent for the way you spend your money?

14. What do these seven qualities (joy, peace, love, light, hope, healing, and the fruit of the Spirit) mean to you?

15. How are they evidenced in your life right now?

16. Which of these qualities do you feel God is calling you to work on in your life?

✢ Recommended Scripture Reading ✢

Matthew 5-7: Jesus' Sermon on the Mount.

⌒ Highlight and consider all of the commandments Jesus gives us in this passage.

⌒ Which characteristic listed in the Beatitudes (Matthew 5:3-11) would you most like to see flourish in your life?

⌒ Which verse especially resonates with your spirit? Why?

About the Author

JOHN PAUL JACKSON HAS been at the forefront of prophetic ministry for more than 20 years. He has authored several books, produced multiple worship recordings, publishes AWE magazine, and has appeared on television broadcasts such as *The 700 Club*, Benny Hinn's *This Is Your Day* broadcast, TBN's *Praise the Lord* broadcast, Cornerstone Television, Daystar Television, and God Digital.

It was his great love for the Body of Christ that prompted John Paul in 1993 to launch Streams Ministries International, a non-profit organization that endeavors to encourage, motivate, and equip individuals to walk in greater maturity, wisdom, character, and holiness. As founder and chairman, John Paul travels extensively around the world teaching on the Art of Hearing God, dreams and visions, and revelatory gifts. As people experience the supernatural power of God in his meetings, lives continue to be transformed.

John Paul and his wife, Diane, have two children and two grandchildren. They live in the beautiful and serene Lake Sunapee region of New Hampshire.

I AM:
365 Names of God

Designed for daily reading and meditation,
John Paul Jackson has collected 365 names of God
that will guide you into becoming a person who
consistently abides in God's presence. God's names
are a disclosure of God Himself. In His name, there
is peace, comfort, provision, healing, and destiny.
When you mediate on a name of God, you will
discover His transforming power. Hardback.

Retail $24.00

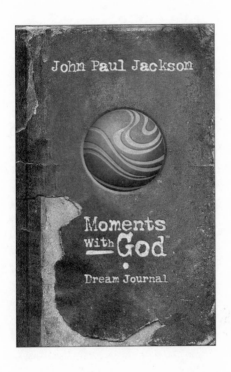

Moments with God Dream Journal

John Paul Jackson shares his unique approach
to dream recording and offers important keys to
unearthing rewarding spiritual insights into your nightly
adventures with God. Included is an easy-to-understand
introduction on dream journaling, three color wheels,
sample journal entries, and specially designed forms
to record your dreams and begin your own personal
dream vocabulary. Hardback.

Retail $24.00

AWE

There's no time like now to try AWE Magazine!
AWE seeks to inspire and empower people in their
quest for a more spiritually fulfilling life.
Each issue of AWE offers insights that are often
startling and always instructive. You'll love AWE
including how it looks. Each issue is visually attractive,
making AWE a treat for the eyes!

**A whole year of inspiration (4 issues)
for only $19.
(Canadian/Foreign $29)**

CD of the Month Club:
Fireside Chats with John Paul Jackson

As a CD of the Month subscriber, you will receive illuminating and inspiring teachings from John Paul Jackson that were recorded during intimate staff gatherings. Topics vary from dreams, portals, and supernatural phenomenon to learning how to exude peace from your spirit. If you are not taking advantage of the personal coaching available from John Paul Jackson, you are missing out.

Annual CD membership only $99.
(Outside the U.S., $115)

I AM: 365 Names of God CD

At the request of many who attended our Xtreme
Moments conferences, John Paul Jackson went into a
studio and read the names of God from his book,
I AM: 365 Names of God. Many can feel the inherent
blessing and increase of faith that happens just from
hearing these names read aloud. Don't miss this
exciting CD from Streams Music Group!

Retail $16.00

Breath of 1 AM CD

Graham Ord's instrumental soundtrack from the
I AM: 365 Names of God CD. Ideal for times of
intercession and therapeutic healing, this soothing
instrumental recording will uplift your spirit
and calm your soul.

Retail $16.00

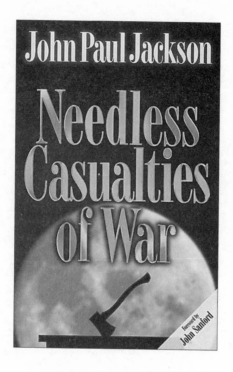

Needless Casualties of War

Unlock the secrets of effective spiritual warfare.
Discover foundational truths that will help you fight
with wisdom and authority. John Paul Jackson offers
a theology of spiritual warfare that is so simple,
yet so profound. Foreword by John Sandford.

Retail $13.00

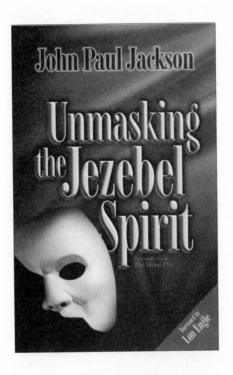

Unmasking the Jezebel Spirit

With keen insight, John Paul Jackson peers through
the enemy's smoke screen and exposes one of the most
deceptive snares used to destroy the Church.
Bibically anchored, this fascinating book is seasoned
with years of personal observation, divine revelation
and thoughtful reflection. Foreword by Lou Engle.

Retail $13.00

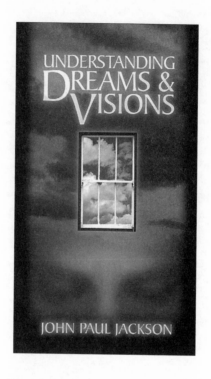

Understanding Dreams and Visions

Explore the world of dreams. Unravel the mysteries of dream interpretation in this inspiring series and discover how to apply God-given insights in your waking life. You don't want to miss these fascinating insights from a gifted dream expert.

(Six audiotapes in an album)

Retail $36.00

Spiritual Dilemmas

Challenging and inspiring, this tape series will
encourage you to find fulfillment in your revelatory
gift. John Paul Jackson reveals how past wounds of
rejection, isolation, guilt, and the tendency to make
comparisons will stifle your prophetic gift.

(Six audiotapes in an album)
Retail $36.00

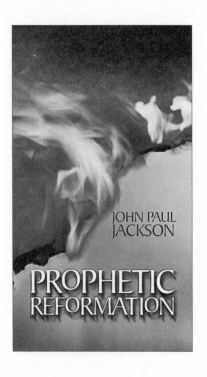

Prophetic Reformation

Discover a fresh perspective on how to increase
your effectiveness as a prophetic person. Join
John Paul Jackson as he explores the need for a
comprehensive change in the way we view
prophetic ministry in the church.

(Six audiotapes in an album)

Retail $36.00

Passage to Intimacy

John Paul Jackson shares compelling stories
about how to bond with God and deepen
your intimacy with the Lord.

(Four audiotapes in an album)

Retail $24.00

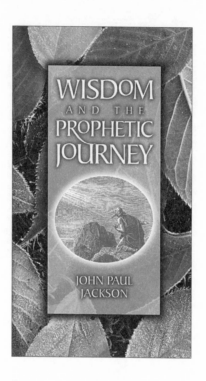

Wisdom and the Prophetic Journey

In clear, simple terms, John Paul Jackson examines
fundamental principles essential to growing in spiritual
maturity. This dynamic series provides insights
into living a truly transformed spirit-filled life
as a revelatory person.

(Two audiotapes in an album)
Retail $12.00

Preparing for Your Visitation

Encounter God's transforming power in your life
like never before. In this life-changing series,
John Paul Jackson uncovers the greatest ploys of the
enemy that have hindered many from truly entering
into God's glorious presence. As you embrace these
truths, you will discover how to prepare for a
supernatural visitation from God.

(Three audiotapes in an album)
Retail $18.00

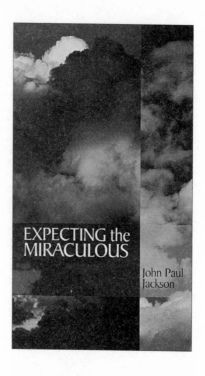

Expecting the Miraculous

Revolutionize the way you think about
impossible and overwhelming situations.
In this inspiring series, John Paul Jackson reveals
how to take difficult situations and transform them
into supernatural adventures. You'll discover
how to change your perceptions and
what it means to be empowered by faith.

(Three audiotapes in an album)
Retail $18.00

Message to America

On September 11, America was brought to its knees. As Americans seek a path toward healing and recovery, John Paul Jackson explains the proper response to the dark events surrounding the terrorist attacks on America and heaven's strategies for the turbulent times ahead.

(*Single audiotape*)
Retail $7.00

Naturally Supernatural

A unique, unedited version of a workshop
that took place in Southampton, England, when
John Paul Jackson chronicled several exciting,
supernatural events. You'll hear hundreds of people
squeal with delight as nearly two dozen heavenly hosts
become visible to the eye, and fly through the room.
Many there were changed forever.

(Single audiotape)
Retail $7.00

Order Form

☞ ORDER ONLINE: **www.streamsministries.com**
☞ CALL TOLL-FREE (U.S. AND CANADA): **1-888-441-8080**
☞ FAX ORDERS TOLL-FREE (U.S. AND CANADA): **1-888-868-8005**
☞ POSTAL ORDERS: **Streams Publications, P.O. Box 550,
North Sutton, NH 03260 USA**

Quantity	Title	Price

SubTotal _____

Shipping and Handling _____

Total This Order _____

(PLEASE PRINT CLEARLY)

NAME:_____

STREET ADDRESS:_____

APT._____ CITY:_____

STATE:_____ ZIP:_____

COUNTRY:_____ PHONE:_____

E-MAIL: _____

METHOD OF PAYMENT:

_____ Check or Money Order (Make check payable to *Streams Ministries*)

_____ Credit Card: ❑ VISA   ❑ MasterCard   ❑ American Express   ❑ Discover

CARD NUMBER:_____-_____-_____-_____   EXPIRATION DATE: _____ / _____

CARD HOLDER (please print):_____

SIGNATURE: _____
   (Credit card orders cannot be processed without signature)

For current shipping and handling information, call 1-888-441-8080.
Or visit our website at www.streamsministries.com.